HIKE
SOUTH BAY

Hike. Contemplate what makes you happy and what makes you happier still. Follow a trail or blaze a new one. **Hike.** Think about what you can do to expand your life and someone else's. **Hike.** Slow down. Gear up. **Hike.** Connect with friends. Re-connect with nature.

Hike. Shed stress. Feel blessed. **Hike** to remember. **Hike** to forget. **Hike** for recovery. **Hike** for discovery. **Hike.** Enjoy the beauty of providence. **Hike.** Share the way, The Hiker's Way, on the long and winding trail we call life.

HIKE
SOUTH BAY

BY
JOHN MCKINNEY

TheTrailmaster.com

HIKE the South Bay By John McKinney

HIKE the South Bay © 2019 The Trailmaster, Inc. All rights reserved. Manufactured in the United States of America. No part of this book may be used or reproduced in any manner whatsoever without written permission except in the case of brief quotations embodied in articles and reviews.

ISBN-13: 978-0-934161-85-5
Book Design by Lisa DeSpain
Cartography by Brandi Webber
Cover photo by Brendan Bane
HIKE Series Editor: Cheri Rae

Published by Olympus Press and The Trailmaster, Inc., TheTrailmaster.com (Visit our site for a complete listing of all Trailmaster publications, products, and services.)

ACKNOWLEDGMENTS: The Trailmaster is most appreciative for the review of his work and cooperation in the field from the dedicated staff of Santa Clara County Parks, MidPeninsula Regional Open Space District (with a special tip of the hiker's cap to docent Karen DeMello), Open Space Authority of Santa Clara Valley, Peninsula Open Space Trust, and Don Edwards San Francisco Bay National Wildlife Refuge.

Although The Trailmaster, Inc. and the author have made every attempt to ensure that information in this book is accurate, they are not responsible for any loss, damage, injury, or inconvenience that may occur to you while using this information. You are responsible for your own safety; the fact that an activity or trail is described in this book does not mean it will be safe for you. Trail conditions can change from day to day; always check local conditions and know your limitations.

Contents

INTRODUCTION 11
ABOUT THE SOUTH BAY 17

I South Bay Classics

Diablo Range

MONUMENT PEAK 25
    Views from the Santa Clara Valley to San Francisco to the High Sierra

ALUM ROCK PARK 29
    The true nature of San Jose in one of California's oldest municipal parks

SIERRA VISTA OPEN SPACE PRESERVE 33
    Stunning views from the eastern foothills of Santa Clara County

JOSEPH D. GRANT COUNTY PARK 37
    Roam pastoral grasslands and oak-studded slopes in the largest county park

South of San Jose

MOUNT MADONNA COUNTY PARK 41
    In the northern Santa Cruz Mountains, redwoods and far-reaching vistas.

Uvas Canyon County Park 45
> Redwoods, waterfalls on Swanson Creek, views from Manzanita Point

Mount Umunhum 49
> Ascend mighty Mt. Um on a brand new trail in Sierra Azul Open Space Preserve

Almaden Quicksilver 53
> Explore the historic Quicksilver Mining District in Santa Clara County's second-largest park

Coyote Valley Open Space Preserve 57
> Twenty miles from downtown San Jose, feels like a hundred

Calero County Park 61
> Great hiking and splendid feeling of isolation not found at other county parks

II Peninsula Parks & Preserves

Stevens Creek 67
> Happy Trails since 1924 in Santa Clara County's first park

Portola Redwoods 71
> Walkabout amidst the tall trees in what some call "Little Basin Redwoods State Park"

Rancho San Antonio 75
> Deer Hollow Farm and beyond via well-traveled and remote trails

Monte Bello 79
> Spirit-uplifting hiking along the high ridges of "Beautiful Mountain"

Skyline Ridge 83
> Atop Skyline Ridge, two sweet little ponds and a path that connects them

Russian Ridge ... 87
  Top wildflower preserve, "10 miles from I-280 and a world apart"

Los Trancos ... 91
  San Andreas Fault Trail probes the curious beauty of earthquake country

Windy Hill ... 95
  Splendid hiking up a windy hill for 360-degree panoramas

Purisima Creek Redwoods ... 99
  Enchanting redwood forest and 20 miles of trail

Huddart Park/Phleger Estate ... 103
  Dense stands of redwoods, deep and steep ravines, a walk on the wild side of Woodside

Burleigh Murray Ranch State Park ... 107
  An old barn, old bridge and other rustic architecture on this ramble back into 19th-century ranch life

III On the Waterfront

South Bay

San Francisco Bay NWR ... 113
  Breezy and easy trails, and birds, birds, birds

Baylands Preserve ... 117
  Palo Alto Baylands, best bird-watching ever

San Mateo Coast

Montara Mountain ... 121
  McNee Ranch State Park

Half Moon Bay ... 125
  Hike Coastside Trail to five bayside beaches

COWELL RANCH 129
   Cowell-Purisima Trail, a heart-stirring length of the
   California Coastal Trail

PESCADERO MARSH 133
   A haven for birds, heaven for bird-watchers

BEAN HOLLOW STATE BEACH 137
   Tide pools, a nature trail and a beach of "beans," multi
   colored polished stones

ABOUT THE AUTHOR 142

> "Find yourself in nature. Take a hike in the mountains east and west of Santa Clara Valley. Discover spirit-enriching natural treasures located close to Silicon Valley but a world apart."
> —John McKinney

HIKE ON.

Take a hike into what feels like Old California, with its rolling hills and its oak groves.

Introduction

The South Bay is more often viewed as a place to work not play. Likely the many well educated and highly motivated people who live in the region are among the most hardworking (perhaps overworked) in the U.S.

All the more reason to take a hike! As if recognizing that South Bay residents need to hit the trail and gain the many health benefits of time spent in nature, the Santa Clara County Parks Department describes its regional parks as, "close to home yet away from the pressures of the valley lifestyle."

HIKE the South Bay offers a selection of the best day hikes in the mountains to the east and the west of the Santa Clara Valley, and a sampling of the natural treasures located near Silicon Valley, but a world apart. This guide features a collection of some of my favorite spirit-enriching nature walks, moderate hikes, and challenging all-day adventures.

So what are you waiting for? Head for hills. Climb Monument Peak and roam the Diablo Range. Make tracks for Monte Bello—"the beautiful mountain" in

Italian—a handsome 2,700-foot high ridge, cut by creeks, greened with grass, cloaked with oak woodlands and fir forests. Meander amidst the redwoods in the Santa Cruz Mountains along the inviting trails in Purisima Creek Redwoods Open Space Preserve.

From South Bay high points, look down at what you left behind. From Eagle Rock in Alum Rock Park, enjoy great clear-day vistas of the Santa Clara Valley, and get a particularly good angle on Levi's Stadium, home of the '49ers. From atop Sierra Vista, view the vast network of roads and highways of metro San Jose and beyond. Climb Windy Hill and gain 360-degree panoramas of the bay and ocean, mountains and metropolis.

Find yourself in nature. In Uvas Canyon Park, enjoy the waterfalls on Swanson Creek, vistas from

Anniversary Trail on Windy Hill: Celebrating the good work of the Peninsula Open Space Trust and Midpeninsula Open Space District.

Introduction

Manzanita Point and redwood groves. Hike the San Andreas Fault Trail in Los Trancos Open Space Preserve and experience the strange beauty of earthquake country. Roam Joseph D. Grant County Park, the county's largest park with 9,522 acres of pastoral grasslands and oak-studded slopes.

And don't miss taking a hike along the very shores of the South Bay. Breezy and easy trails and stellar bird-watching await you at The Baylands and at San Francisco Bay National Wildlife Refuge.

I've had the pleasure of hiking around the South Bay for decades. Like many others, I've been amazed—and at times even overwhelmed—by the region's economic boom and burgeoning population. At last count, the South Bay is headquarters for more than 6,500 high-tech companies.

San Jose is the largest city by far in the South Bay, and most populous in the whole Bay Area. Few Americans seem to realize that San Jose is now the tenth-most populous city in the U.S.

Fortunately for the hikers who are part of the two million or so residents of the San Jose-Sunnyvale-Santa Clara metropolitan area, government agencies and nonprofit organizations have created dozens of quality parks and preserves and constructed many miles of trails. Let's give a shout-out to the Santa Clara County Parks Department, and another to the Midpeninsula Open Space District, the latter offering a great collection of more than two dozen regional parklands, as well as pathways that literally and figuratively link the Peninsula and South Bay.

I've been pleased to observe an ever-increasing number of hikers, as well as improved pathways, park facilities and visitor/interpretive centers around the South Bay. Let us give thanks for the significant number of parks in the region that are "hiker parks"—parks with a minimum of facilities and excellent trail systems.

By strict definition, the South Bay is the southern region of the San Francisco Bay Area, most particularly the Santa Clara Valley. While the South Bay is nearly synonymous with Santa Clara County, the northern part of the county—Palo Alto, Los Altos, Mountain View—is often considered part of the Peninsula.

The definition of the South Bay, at least as a place to live, work, and hike, is much more fluid than that of the East Bay for example. Everyone defines the East Bay as Alameda and Contra Costa counties and that's that. What might be a strictly geographic definition of the South Bay has been altered by the geography of Silicon Valley and the high-tech job market.

Bay Area media professionals, particularly technology writers and pundits, offer highly expansive definitions of the South Bay that include Santa Cruz County (and sometimes way beyond that!) and also include East Bay cities such as Fremont (considered part of Silicon Valley and therefore part of the South Bay).

Introduction

Peninsula communities that are so much a part of Silicon Valley are commonly included in references to the South Bay. Longtime Peninsula residents get annoyed when Mountain View and Palo Alto are referred to as part of the South Bay. The Trailmaster understands your vexation: Mountain View, for example, has always been part of the Peninsula and just because it's at the heart of the Silicon Valley doesn't mean it got relocated to the South Bay.

What we now call Silicon Valley was an agricultural region from the time of the Gold Rush to World War II. Enter the electronics and aerospace industries. Adios to (much) agriculture. Santa Clara Valley, aka Silicon Valley, became the top technology center of the U.S. and the valley was transformed into an urbanized metropolis. Many towns along the Peninsula experienced a similar development pattern: they were rural enclaves as well until the 1950s when large numbers of families settled here. From the 1980s on, the Peninsula population has grown exponentially in tandem with the technology boom of Silicon Valley.

Friends and fellow hikers have half-seriously suggested this guide be titled "HIKE Silicon Valley" because the featured hikes are ones that appeal to those who live and work in the region. No doubt the South Bay has more than its share of that species of hiker known as the High-Tech Trekker, defined by the *Urban Dictionary* as "an individual who enjoys outdoor activities, enjoys nature and is an environmentalist. Is NOT a hippie due to their enthusiasm for new technology and is an avid consumer of anything to do with innovation, from computers to high-performance equipment."

Sound like anyone you know?

While hiking the South Bay trails featured in this guide, I observed some of the best-equipped hikers I've ever seen during my 30 years on the trail. I also encountered many hikers carrying only the most basic gear, and those who told me they love hiking for the opportunity to "unplug."

Whether you're a High-Tech Trekker or embrace the philosophy of the great naturalist Henry David Thoreau ("Beware of all enterprises that require new clothes"), it's easy to get away in the South Bay. Hiking season is winter, spring, summer, and fall. Yes, the South Bay offers four-season hiking!

Discover the natural world nearby. Enjoy the rich diversity of hikes in the hills, mountains and bay lands around the South Bay and the many inviting pathways along the Peninsula.

Hike smart, reconnect with nature and have a wonderful time on the trail.

Hike On.

John McKinney

South Bay

Geography

From the southern edge of San Francisco Bay, the Santa Clara Valley extends south between two coastal mountain ranges. Known for decades as "Valley of Heart's Delight," the valley once abounded in orchards and, until the 1960s, was the largest fruit production and packing region in the world.

Most of Santa Clara Valley, including San Jose, lies within Santa Clara County. The northern (and quite urbanized) part of the long valley is commonly known as the South Bay, and known worldwide as the famed tech industry region, Silicon Valley.

Bordering Santa Clara Valley to the east is the Diablo Range, topped by Mt. Hamilton and Monument Peak. On the west side of the valley lie the Santa Cruz Mountains.

The term "Peninsula" could refer to the whole San Francisco Peninsula. However by popular use the city of San Francisco at the north end of the peninsula is excluded and the Peninsula refers to cities south of the city.

Natural History

The diversity of South Bay topography from valley floor to mountains accounts for a variety of flora from the chaparral and coastal sage scrub communities on sunny slopes to oak-dotted meadows to conifers, including redwoods, in the mountains.

In Monte Bello Open Space Preserve, Stevens Creek Nature Trail tours a variety of landscapes from grassland to chaparral to evergreen forest. That kind of variety of plant communities is common in Santa Clara County parks and the Midpeninsula Open Space preserves.

Sometimes the nature preserves seem like islands on the land. "Ten miles from I-280 and a world apart." That's one way to describe Russian Ridge Open Space Preserve, a top locale to enjoy wildflower displays—prodigious bursts of blossoms—fields of lupine and poppies, plus cream cups, owl's clover, mule's ear and more.

A Mediterranean climate nurtures Mediterranean flora—and more, including mixed woodlands and gray pines growing at 2,000 feet or so in elevation on Mt. Umunhum in Sierra Azul Open Space Preserve.

Conservation History

San Jose has long promoted its environmental consciousness while facing the challenges of trying to reduce the effects of urban/suburban sprawl. The city and surrounding communities have managed to limit development in some areas and preserve open space and parklands in the nearby hills. Alum Rock, one of California's oldest municipal parks, was founded in 1872.

Located just 20 miles from downtown San Jose, Coyote Valley Open Space Preserve, which opened in 2015 was at the center of a decades-long dispute and is symbolic of the struggle between the competing needs for industrial space and open space. Is the valley a primo location for more high-tech industry? Or is it a natural treasure that should be preserved?

Santa Clara County Parks acquired its first park in 1924 and the park system now numbers 28 regional

Orchards and open space: How the Santa Clara Valley used to look.

parks. In 1994 Santa Clara County Open Space Authority (SCOSA) was formed to preserve land and create parks (see Coyote Valley and Sierra Vista hike descriptions) in the south part of Santa Clara County.

Midpeninsula Regional Open Space District, self-described as "a regional greenbelt system near busy Silicon Valley," was established in 1972. More than 220 miles of trail lead through the District's diverse collection of 26 open space preserves.

Administration: Contact the Santa Clara County Parks and Recreation Department, sometimes referred to as Santa Clara County Parks Department or Santa Clara County Parks at 408-355-2200 or visit parkhere.org.

Twenty miles of trail lead through enchanting Purisima Creek Redwoods OSP.

For info about the Midpeninsula Regional Open Space District call 650-691-1200 or visit openspace. org Reach The Open Space Authority of Santa Clara Valley at 408-224-7476 or visit openspaceauthority. org. Contact the Don Edwards San Francisco Bay National Wildlife Refuge at 510-792-0222 or visit fws.gov/refuge/Don_Edwards_San_Francisco_Bay.

Transit to Trails: For bus and rail maps and schedules contact the Santa Clara Valley Transportation Authority at vta.org

Hit the trail to Monument Peak
from Ed R. Levin Park.

EVERY TRAIL TELLS A STORY.

I
South Bay Classics

HIKE ON.

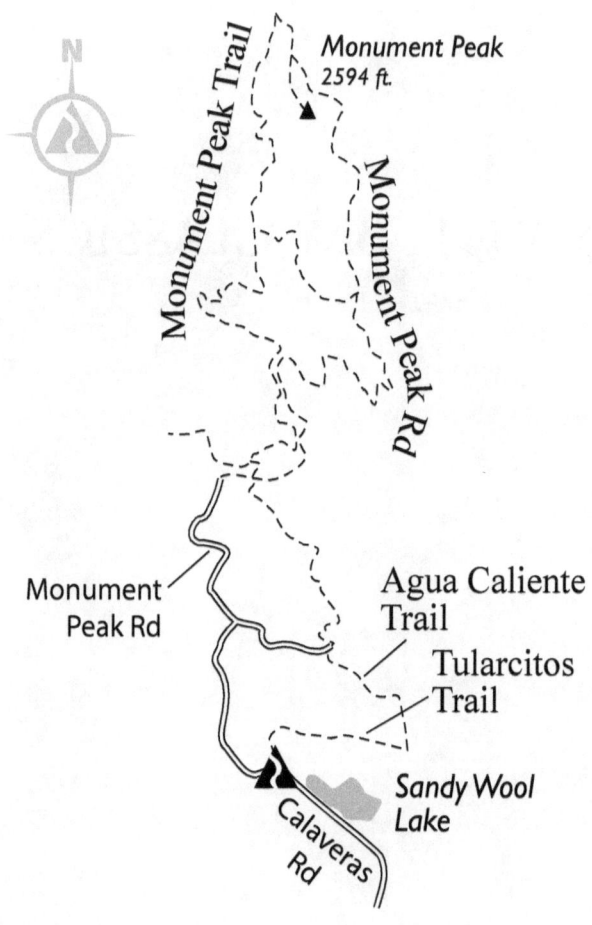

Monument Peak

Tularcitos, Agua Caliente, Monument Peak Trails

To summit of Monument Peak is 8 miles round trip with 2,000-foot elevation gain

Monument Peak is much too much a monumental undertaking for most visitors to Ed R. Levin County Park. A round of golf at the attractive Spring Valley Golf Course, fishing for bass and blue gill at Sandy Wool Lake, an off-leash dog park, picnicking and playing on the wide lawns—these are the chief attractions here.

Only hikers enjoy the panoramic view from the 2,594-foot peak, a view some reckon is nearly equal to that from atop Mt. Hamilton. Vistas from the Santa Clara Valley to San Francisco Bay to the High Sierra are the hiker's reward for gaining the summit.

Located on the border between Alameda and Santa Clara counties, Monument Peak is part of a ridge in the Diablo Range that also includes nearby

Mission Peak. While not exactly undiscovered, Monument Peak attracts fewer hikers than other Bay Area high points.

Hang-gliders get a hawk's-eye-view of the park named for Ed R. Levin, a geologist and county planning commissioner who was instrumental in securing it. The park has expanded to 1,541 acres and includes a two-mile long valley and a bordering ridge that rises to Monument Peak.

DIRECTIONS: From Highway 680 in Milpitas, exit on Calaveras Road and drive 2 miles east to Ed R. Levin County Park. Join Tularcitos Trail at the northwest (upper) parking area of Sandy Wool Lake near the dog park.

THE HIKE: From Tularcitos Trailhead, the path ascends 0.5 mile to Agua Caliente Trail. Turn north and climb steeply, soon gaining stellar views of Sandy Wool Lake and what are surprisingly grand vistas of the South Bay so early into the hike.

After passing a hang-glider launch site and a junction with Higuera Trail, Agua Caliente Trail continues a switchbacking ascent to trail junction at the 1.5-mile mark. Turn right on Monument Peak Trail. Cross Monument Peak Road and start a steep route toward the summit.

As the trail nears Calera Creek, scattered oaks and some cottonwood offers some relief from the mostly shadeless ascent. The path crosses the head of Calera Creek (where there's a small dammed pond) and meets Monument Peak Road. Take the road, passing right-forking Sierra Trail that leads to an aerie hang-gliding launch. Follow the road to the park boundary just below the summit.

Retrace your steps or descend Monument Peak Road back to Agua Caliente. For a bit more variety, hike back down Monument Peak Road to a four-way junction to meet Monument Peak Trail and Agua Caliente Trail and hike the latter. Join Agua Caliente Trail, a dirt road that's also part of the Bay Area Ridge Trail.

Make a mellow ascent to Peak 2543 (only 50 feet lower than Monument Peak). Grab great Bay views, then descend rapidly to a wooded canyon. The park crosses Scott Creek, climbs out of the canyon then descends again, Pass junctions with Calera Creek Trail and Monument Peak Trail and retrace your steps to the trailhead.

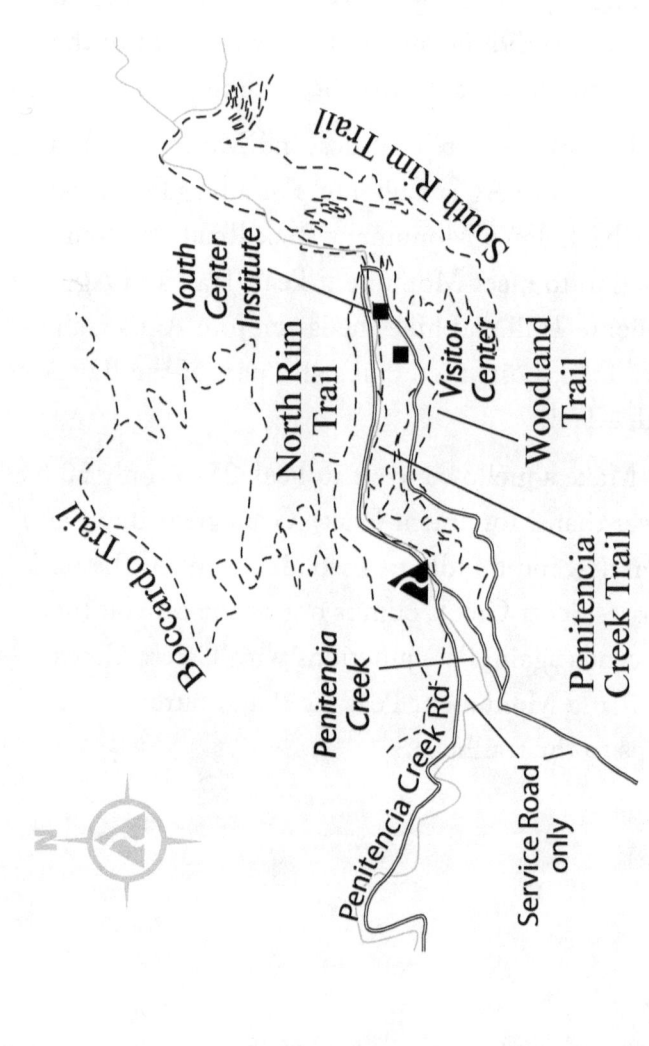

ALUM ROCK PARK

CREEK, SOUTH RIM TRAILS

4 miles round trip with 600-foot elevation gain.

San Jose citizens have been flocking to Alum Rock, one of California's oldest municipal parks, since the park was founded in 1872. In the 1890s, the park's mineral waters were tapped to become a Euro-style health spa complete with baths, indoor swimming pool, tea garden, and dance pavilion. Public transit was terrific: one could board the Alum Rock Railroad in downtown San Jose and ride to the resort for just 25 cents!

The resort is long gone (closed in 1932), and suburbs have sprawled toward the park's boundaries, but Santa Clara Valley residents still enjoy hiking in what used to be known as "The Reservation." Park highlight is the tranquil canyon of Penitencia Creek, traveled by wide Creek Trail (honored with National Recreation Trail designation).

Trails lead past namesake Alum Rock (625 feet); the name arose from the mistaken belief there was aluminum in the rocks. A short trail ascends Eagle Rock (795 feet), not exactly an alpine summit, but certainly scenic! Eagle Rock is a great promontory for a picnic and to savor clear-day views of the Santa Clara Valley, San Jose, and, for football fans, a particularly good angle on Levi's Stadium, home of the 49ers. Watch for red-tailed hawks and turkey vultures soaring overhead.

The park has a network of 13 miles of trails; equestrians and cyclists are restricted to certain trails while hikers can use all the pathways. Alum Park trails connect to an adjacent system of Santa Clara Open Space Authority trails.

Enjoy what may be the classic Alum Rock Park hike: Travel with Creek Trail along Penitencia Creek, then climb South Rim Trail to several excellent vista points.

DIRECTIONS: From I-680, exit on Berryessa Road East. Turn right on Capitol Avenue, then left on Penitencia Creek Road to Alum Rock Park (entry fee). Park in the lot below the entry kiosk and join Penitencia Creek Trail. If the lot is full, continue to one of the picnic areas and access the trail from any of several points in the main part of the park.

THE HIKE: From the parking lot, cross a bridge and head up-creek on Creek Trail. Pass seeping springs and grottos of mineral-covered rocks. The Penitencia Creek corridor is shaded by alder, sycamore and big-leaf maple. Cross a stone bridge, and then a steel one over the creek.

Continue through the shady environs, no doubt in good and plentiful company, to meet hikers-only South Rim Trail. Ascend a series of switchbacks amidst oak and bay. Near the rim, a short connector trail leads to an isolated picnic area.

Hike along the rim across open and sunny slopes amidst toyon and other chaparral flora. Pass a junction with Switchback Trail (which drops to the canyon floor). South Rim Trail bends north and zigzags down to the creek and canyon near the visitor center and Youth Science Institute.

Founded in 1872, Alum Rock Park once featured a popular European-style health spa; the trail leads past reminders of that era.

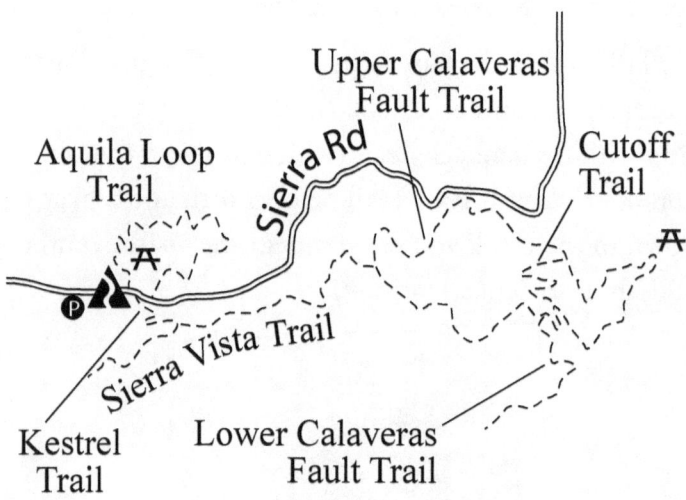

Sierra Vista
Open Space Preserve

Sierra Vista, Upper Calaveras Fault Trails Council

4.5 miles round trip with 700-foot elevation gain

As a place name "Sierra Vista" won't win any awards for originality, but it's an accurate description for this preserve in the eastern foothills of Santa Clara County that offers visitors stunning views of the greater South Bay. The vista takes in Levi's Stadium, Moffett Field, the Dunbarton Bridge, downtown San Jose, Mt. Hamilton and the Lick Observatory, and even Jacks Peak way off on the Monterey Peninsula.

For a dozen years Sierra Vista OSP was accessible only by way of a stiff climb of an hour or more from Alum Rock Park. One did not make a casual visit only a calculated one to Sierra Vista. Then in 2014 the Open Space Authority constructed a trailhead and parking area at the top of Sierra Road. (Most everybody loves the new trailhead though there are a few purists who regard such easy access as "cheating.")

Two new trails were built and now 11 miles of trail cross the 1,898-acre mountainous preserve. Aquila Loop Trail (1.2 miles) offers an easy intro to the preserve. Kestrel Trail (0.25 mile) links Aquila Loop with Sierra Vista Trail. Vistas from these trails are extraordinary: the dramatic canyon cut by Penitencia Creek, and South Bay to the max: metro San Jose and the southern portion of San Francisco Bay from Mountain View to south San Jose.

Expect to share the preserve with cows. Cattle grazing is part of the preserve's management plan to reduce invasive plants, restore native flora and reduce the risk of wildfire. When a fire started in the summer of 2016, it was limited to 5 acres; that the fire didn't spread rapidly was due to the swift action of firefighters and the grazing practices that had reduced the fuel load in the preserve.

DIRECTIONS: From I-680 northbound in San Jose, exit on Berryessa Road. Stay right at a fork and drive 0.25 miles, following the signs for Berryessa Road East. Join Sierra Road and proceed 6.5 miles northeast on the winding road to the Sierra Vista OSP trailhead and parking area.

THE HIKE: As you begin, behold the contrasting vistas: the vast network of roads and highways of metro San Jose and the impressive gorge cut by Penitencia Creek through the Diablo Range.

Kestrel Trail leads 0.25 mile to Sierra Vista Trail. Bear left and enjoy a mellow contour across slopes high, high above Penitencia Creek. A mile out, reach a junction with Upper Calaveras Fault Trail (your return route). Stay right with Sierra Vista Trail and descend very steeply, past an old ranch house to meet uip again with Upper Calaveras Fault Trail (the fire road is known as "Lower Calaveras Fault Trail" in the southeastern part of the preserve).

Up you go, regaining all that elevation and more as the trail leads west near Sierra Road then returns to meet Sierra Vista Trail. Retrace your steps a mellow mile back to the trailhead.

Get above all: Sierra Vista delivers views of the South Bay metropolis below.

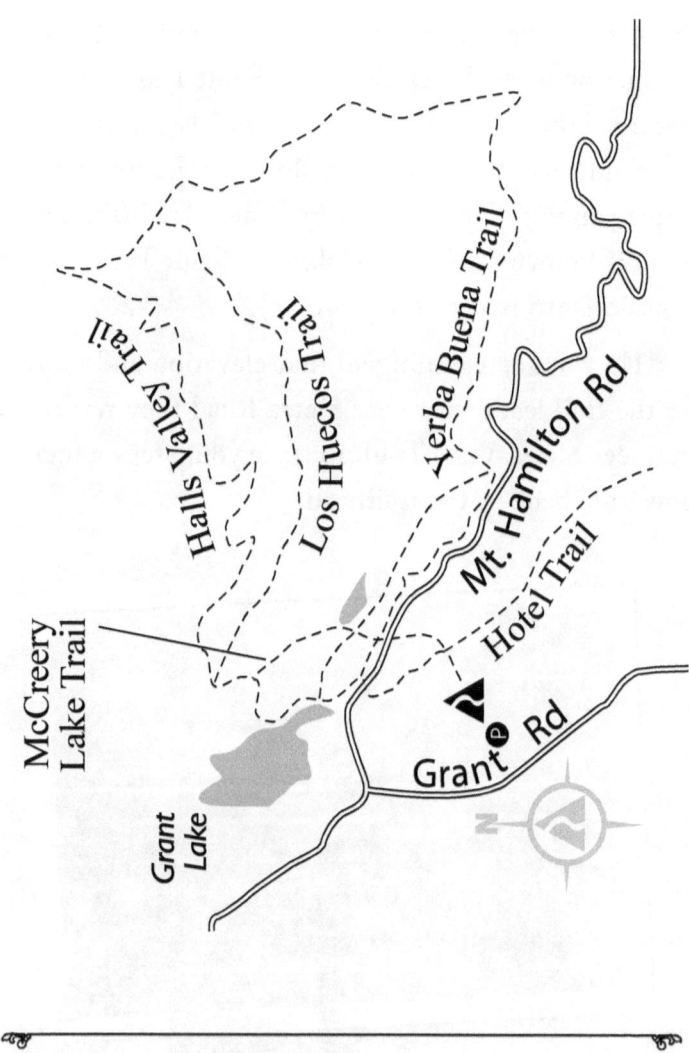

Joseph D. Grant County Park

Hotel, Yerba Buena, Canada de Pala, Halls Valley Trails

7.5 miles round trip with 1,100-foot elevation gain

Tucked between two ridges in the Diablo Mountains lies Halls Valley, pastoral ranching country that's the centerpiece of Joseph D. Grant County Park. The onetime haunts of the native Ohlone and former Mexican land grant is now the county's largest park with 9,522 acres of pastoral grasslands and oak-studded slopes.

As you roam the foothills of Mt. Hamilton, it's hard to believe this park is only 15 miles from downtown San Jose!

Adam Grant purchased the land in 1880. His son, park namesake Joseph Donohoe Grant, enjoyed getaways to the ranch and was also a civic minded city-dweller—a San Francisco arts patron and a founder of the Save-the-Redwoods League. The family ranch house hosts a museum with nature exhibits and displays from the ranching era.

Forty miles of trail, mostly old ranch roads, weave through Halls Valley and head into the surrounding hills. Best introduction to the park's charms is a loop through Halls Valley, named for 19th-century attorney and local historian Frederick Hall. Use connector trails to shorten or lengthen the hike.

DIRECTIONS: From Interstate 680 in San Jose, exit on Alum Rock Avenue and drive 4 miles east to Mt. Hamilton Road. Turn right and travel 8 miles on the twisty road to the entrance of Joseph D. Grant County Park (fee). Continue past the first parking lot and veer left to another lot and the trailhead for Hotel Trail.

THE HIKE: Join signed Hotel Trail (paved at its very beginning), soon staying straight and passing by the historic Halls family ranch buildings, and in 0.1 mile go left at a junction and stick with wide Hotel Trail as it climbs 0.3 mile to Mt. Hamilton Road. Cross the road to meet Yerba Buena Trail and go right.

The trail ascends on mostly shade-less slopes alongside Mt. Hamilton Road and enters a cattle range. Pass a junction with McCreery Lake Trail on the left. At 1.2 miles, the trail parts company with the road and ascends a bit eastward. Look back west for a view of Bass Lake.

At 2.6 miles, meet Canada de Pala Trail and head right (west), ascending to the hike's high point (about 2,600 feet) and a bench. Enjoy views back to the trailhead and well beyond to metro San Jose.

Onward, across a cattle range, get views of Mt. Hamilton and the Lick Observatory and reach a junction with Halls Valley Trail at 4.3 miles. Go left and make a moderate descent across grassland with drifts of valley oaks.

About 6.3 miles out, pass junctions with Los Huecos and Canal Trails. Continue past more oaks and even some eucalyptus, cross a creek and meet Yerba Buena Trail. Hike along the shore of Grant Lake past a parking area and picnic area. Cross Mt. Hamilton Road to rejoin Hotel Trail and retrace your steps to the trailhead.

Great hiking at Grant Park, 15 miles from downtown San Jose and a world apart.

TheTrailmaster.com

Mount Madonna County Park

Merry-Go Round, Ridge Trails

Loop is 4.6 miles round trip with 1,200 foot elevation gain

At the turn of the 20th century, Henry Miller (the Central California cattle baron not the California literary lion) built a summer home on the cool shoulders of Mt. Madonna in order to escape the searing heat of his considerable kingdom below. It was said that everywhere Miller looked from on high he could see land that belonged to him—a million acres at the time of his death in 1916.

Some historians credit the Italian craftsmen in Miller's employ for naming the mountain after the Virgin Mary; others contend the Madonna moniker came from a local recluse poet named Hiram Wentworth.

Today, Miller's mountaintop is in public domain, a 4,605-acre county park offering camping, picnicking, fishing at Sprig Lake and 14 miles of trail that explore the canyons and ridgetops. Centerpiece of the park is namesake Mt. Madonna, the 1,897-foot high point of the southern Santa Cruz Mountains.

From the slopes of Mt. Madonna, enjoy great vistas to the east of Santa Clara Valley and to the west all the way to Monterey Bay.

Madonna is more than just another redwood park. Topography and vegetation vary and hikers have the opportunity here to wander from oak woodland to grassland to chaparral clad slopes. And of course, there are redwoods en route.

The trail network is a complication of footpaths, retired logging roads and powerline service roads. The park map can be a big help because trail junctions are numerous. While it's hard to get really lost, it's easy to miss the trail connection you're seeking. The suggested loop is just that: a suggestion. It's easy to add more mileage to this hike, and you can take a little shortcut on Tie Camp Trail to shorten it.

This hikes begins a little bit away from the main part of the park at Sprig Lake on the eastern slopes of Mt. Madonna.

DIRECTIONS: From Highway 101 in Gilroy, exit on Highway 152 West and drive 7 miles west to Mt. Madonna County Park. Turn right at the sign for Sprig Lake. Park in the lot or along the access road. Walk 250 feet up a gravel road to the trailhead.

THE HIKE: From the end of the road at the Sprig Lake trailhead, observe two fire roads and choose the right one—Merry-Go-Round Trail. Ascend along a seasonal creek and through a mixed woodland of coastal live oak, sycamore, madrone, and California bay. With the moderate to steep climb, come even more trees to behold: valley oak, big-leaf maple, and yes, redwoods.

About 1.2 miles out, pass a junction with Old Mine Trail on your right. Continue the ascent another 0.2 mile over brushy slopes to a junction with Tie Camp Trail (a shortcut over to the Ridge Trail if you'd like to shorten this loop hike).

More climbing, steeper now, amidst madrone, tanoak and redwoods to a junction at about the 1.9 mile-mark with Tan Oak Trail. For our loop hike, continue straight on Loop Trail. The route levels out for a time, passes junctions with Lower Miller and Upper Miller trails, then follows a line of utility poles to meet Ridge Trail about 2.5 miles from the trailhead.

Go left on Ridge Trail, which bends this way and that, as you follow it on a moderate to steep descent through the woods and over chaparral-covered slopes. When the trail pops into the open, look east for the hills of Henry Coe State Park, at 89,614 acres the second-largest of our 280 California State Parks.

Continue with Ridge Trail past all junctions (with Contour Trail, Tie Camp Trail, Blackhawk Trail) back to the trailhead.

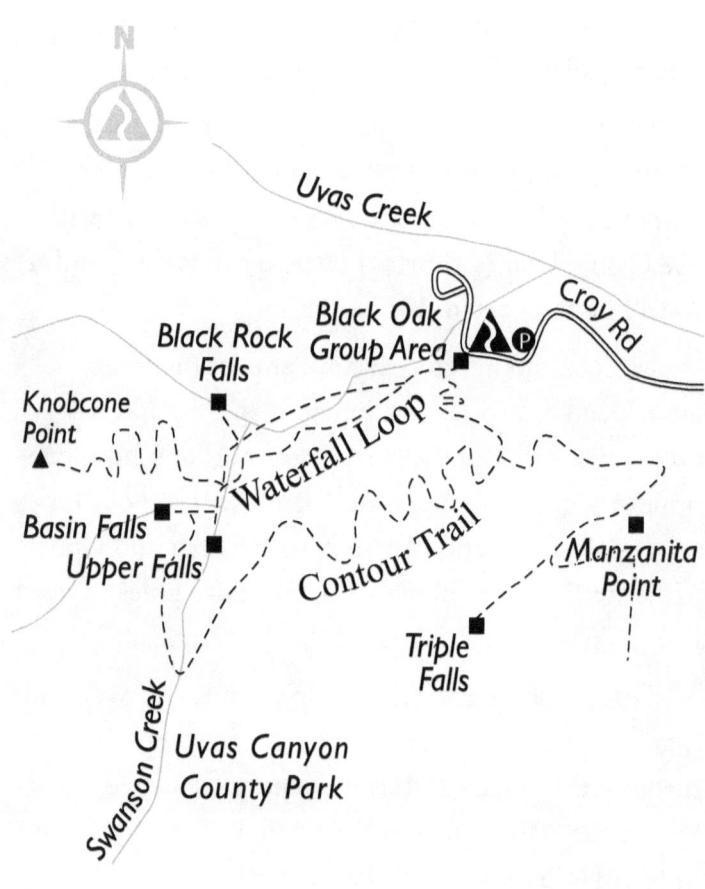

Uvas Canyon County Park

Waterfall Loop, Contour, Alec Canyon Trails

4-mile loop with 700-foot elevation gain.

Three waterfalls on Swanson Creek, views from Manzanita Point and redwood groves are among the highlights of Uvas Canyon County Park. Trails explore the cool, heavily forested canyons and brushy, sun-baked ridgetops.

Most ambitious hike in the park is the stiff two-mile climb (with 1,800-foot elevation gain) to Nibbs Knob. Views of the Diablo Range and Santa Clara Valley compensate you for the vigorous climb.

But the hiking here is really all about getting to the waterfalls. This moderately easy loop along Swanson Creek and Alec Canyon visits several waterfalls. Late winter and spring—when the rain-swollen Swanson Creek cascades are at their most vigorous—are particularly fine times to take this hike.

DIRECTIONS: From Highway 85 in San Jose, exit on the Almaden Expressway and drive 5 miles south to its end. Turn right on Harry Road, make a quick left onto McKean Road, and drive south 6.5 miles; the road continues as Uvas Road 3.5 more miles to Croy Road. Turn right and drive 3.8 miles to road's end at the entry to Uvas Canyon Park. Find the trailhead at Black Oak Group Picnic Area and parking near the park entrance/ranger station.

THE HIKE: From the lot, climb stairs to the restrooms and walk up the park road to where it splits. Alec Canyon Trail leads straight ahead but for now, bear left, following signs for Waterfall Loop Trail (a dirt road) that begins at a gate.

After 0.1 mile, the dirt road continues above the north bank of Swanson Creek, while a footpath travels in the company of maples and tanbark oaks on the south side of the creek, crossing it twice; the routes reunite in 0.25 mile.

About 0.5 mile out, meet a short spur trail that leads to well-named Black Rock Falls, in a magical, mossy setting. The blue-flowered myrtle (aka periwinkle) is common on the hillsides around here.

Soon reach another spur trail branching west to Knobcone Point. The main trail leads a short distance farther to turnoffs for Upper Falls, the park's highest, and to Basin Falls, a 15-foot cascade, both products of nearby Swanson Creek.

Crossing Swanson Creek, the path joins Contour Trail, which contours across steep slopes amidst a mixed forest of oaks, bay, madrone and Douglas fir. After 1.25 miles, the path ends at a junction with Alec Canyon Trail.

Ascend the narrow path 0.2 mile through the canyon to Manzanita Point and peer out over the manzanita for a view dominated by Mt. Hamilton and the Diablo Range. Continue south, first across brushy slopes, then into cool redwoods. A short jaunt on right-forking Triple Falls Trail brings you to a trio of cascades (about 40 feet total) on Alec Creek.

Retrace your steps to the junction with Contour Trail and continue on Alec Canyon Trail on a 0.4-mile descent back to Black Oak Picnic Area and the trailhead.

Waterfall Loop Trail leads to three lovely waterfalls on Swanson Creek.

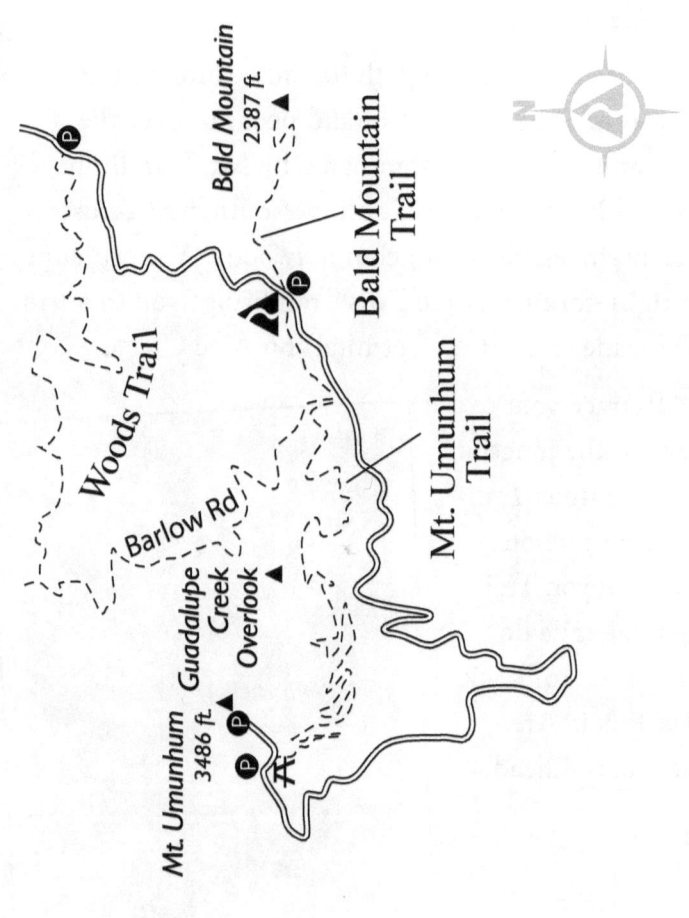

Mount Umunhum

Mt. Umunhum Trail

To Guadalupe Creek Overlook is 2.6 miles round trip with 350-foot elevation gain; to summit is 7.4 miles round trip with 1,150-foot gain

Closed to hikers for many years, the summit of Mount Umunhum re-opened in 2017, and rejoined the ranks of other great Bay Area peaks, such as Mt. Tamalpais and Mt. Diablo, that are accessible to the public and offer spectacular views.

Mount Umunhum is topped by a concrete radar tower, a relic of the Cold War. The U.S. Air Force built the facility in the 1950s to detect any hostile Soviet military action and operated it until 1979.

Mount Umunhum is part of the Sierra Azul or "Blue Range," a chain of promontories with a bluish haze. The prominent 3,486-foot peak is the centerpiece of the huge Sierra Azul Open Space Preserve, set aside in 1983 and expanded over the years to 18,000 acres.

Long before it was the site of Alamden Air Force Station, the mountain offered a place of prayer for Native Americans. Umunhum comes from the native Ohlone and translates to "resting place of the hummingbird."

Midpeninsula Regional Open Space District obtained Congressional funds to clean up the summit and other public funds to spearhead lengthy restoration efforts to environmentally rehabilitate the mountaintop (that had been flattened by the military), as well as build viewpoints, picnic areas, and the new Mt. Umunhum Trail that leads to the summit from the Bald Mountain parking area/trailhead.

The multi-use trail offers a fine intro to the varied terrain of the sprawling preserve, crosses three impressive steel bridges, and features the highest point on the Bay Area Ridge Trail. Reward for the climb are views from Monterey Bay to all around San Francisco Bay, from Santa Cruz to the High Sierra.

DIRECTIONS: From Highway 85 in San Jose, exit on Camden Avenue and go south 2 miles. Turn right on Hicks Road and drive 6.4 miles to Mt. Umunhum Road. Turn right and travel 1.7 miles to the Bald Mountain Parking Area.

THE HIKE: Cross the road, join the signed trail, and begin a moderate ascent across slopes densely covered in chamise, manzanita, mountain mahogany, and other chaparral flora. After a mile, cross the first bridge (East Bridge) and at the 1.3-mile mark reach Guadalupe Creek Overlook. Enjoy excellent vistas of the Santa Clara Valley, Mt. Hamilton, and Mt. Diablo.

Continue a mostly mellow climb under the cool canopy of a mixed woodland of oak, bay, and madrone. At 1.9 miles, cross a second bridge (Central Bridge) and, shortly thereafter, at the 2-mile mark, cross a third span (West Bridge). The trail leads upward through the woods and amidst stands of knobcone pine, approaching the cliffs and rocky outcroppings near the summit. Serpentine rock and soil nurture "rock gardens" of rare native flora.

Just short of the summit, the path splits: the multi-use route continues to a weather shelter while a hiker-only trail leads 0.2 mile to the East Summit. Stroll along the easy-access Summit Loop Trail and enjoy the 360-degree vistas.

Hike to the summit of Mount Um to get an up-close view of this monolithic relic of the Cold War.

Almaden Quicksilver

Senador Mine, Guadalupe Mine Trails

4-mile loop with 700-foot elevation gain.

Roam the meadows and oak woodlands of Capitancillos Ridge and explore the historic quicksilver mining district in Almaden Quicksilver County Park, Santa Clara County's second-largest park.

For a time, the quicksilver mines burrowed into six-mile long Los Capitancillo Ridge were the world's most productive. Quicksilver (mercury) mining lacked the glamour of gold mining, but played an important supporting role in California's Gold Rush. Gold miners used quicksilver in the reduction of gold ore.

The ridges and canyons are quiet now. Shafts and tunnels are sealed. Gone are the camps and communities of Mexican, Cornish and Chinese miners. Gone are the more than 500 houses built on Los Capitancillo Ridge. Even the teahouse pagoda sent by a satisfied customer—the emperor of China—is long gone.

What's left are mining ruins, the grassy, steep, oak-studded ridge, and a network of former mining roads that explore the quicksilver country. Some 34 miles of trail wind through the 4,163-acre park.

The New Almaden Quicksilver Mining Museum is located in the Casa Grande (big house) at 21350 Almaden Road. The museum features collections and displays about the history of mercury mining and nearby mining communities.

The park's main (east) entrance is off Almaden Road, where you'll find park headquarters and access to the eastern terminus of the Mine Hill Trail. Popular McAbee Road entrance on the park's north side puts the greatest diversity of trails and terrain at the hiker's feet.

Best short loop and intro to park is via Senador Mine and Guadalupe Trails. The oak woodland en route offers the hiker welcome shade. Get the lay of the land and return, perhaps for a 10- or 12-mile jaunt into the more rugged and remote southern half of the park.

The hike visits the site of the Senador (Senator in English) Mine, which produced lots of quicksilver during its 19th-century heyday and was revived and modernized in the 1920s; left behind from this latter mining era are tall concrete towers, remains of mine's enormous furnace.

DIRECTIONS: From Highway 85 in San Jose, exit on Camden Ave and drive south to McAbee

Road. Turn right and follow it a few blocks to its end at Whispering Pines Drive and park along the neighborhood streets.

THE HIKE: Close to the trailhead, Mine Hill Trail branches leftward, but you join the service road leading to the Senador Mine. After visiting the furnace plant and scanning the interpretive signs, continue uphill on Senador Mine Trail, an old road that climbs to an oak-studded saddle to meet Guadalupe Trail, which you join for a westward descent toward Guadalupe Creek. Alas the creek here is just outside the park boundary and not accessible.

The path leaves the creek and ascends toward Guadalupe Dam, creator of the 1.5-mile long reservoir behind it. At a saddle meet and join Mine Hill Trail, turning left for the return through oak woodland and grassy meadows back to the trailhead.

Hike Quicksilver country: where mining ruins, meadows and oak woodlands combine for a unique adventure.

COYOTE VALLEY

HEART'S DELIGHT, ARROWHEAD LOOP TRAILS

4 miles round trip with 600-foot elevation gain

Twenty miles from downtown San Jose and a world apart, Coyote Valley offers a countryside still grazed by cows and a new, quiet, and peaceful park.

Coyote Valley Open Space Preserve, which opened in 2015, offers 348 acres of rolling, oak-dotted hills. Vistas from the grassy ridges are terrific and include Mt. Umunhun, Mt. Hamilton, and of course the Coyote Valley.

Ah, Coyote Valley, a rural and remarkably unspoiled expanse of farms, fields and orchards along Highway 101 between San Jose and Morgan Hill. Thanks to rich soil, ample water and a year-around growing season, the valley has, for a century or more, produced delicious apricots, cherries, plums and pears.

However, Coyote Valley's fate has been in dispute for decades: Is the valley a prime location for more high-tech industry? Or is it a natural treasure that should be preserved in a region already overwhelmed by industrial developments and urban-suburban sprawl?

In the 1980s, Apple and other companies considered constructing a new headquarters in the Coyote Valley. In 1999, Cisco proposed building an enormous campus for 20,000 employees close to where the preserve is now located.

Conservationists hope that Silicon Valley's newest parkland will be the first of many similar parklands created in the area. Considering Coyote Valley OSP is located within reach of two million people, it's attracted relatively few visitors so far. Parking is usually plentiful and you just might hike the whole loop trail without encountering any other trail-users.

Grasslands display a golden beauty in autumn and in winter/early spring glow emerald green. Watch for deer and coyotes waving through the grass and raptors soaring overhead.

The trail system is mostly one trail/route. Considering it's multi-use and open to horseback riders and mountain bike riders, newly built Arrowhead Trail is surprisingly a single-track pathway. You can take jaunts of 1.7 miles, 3.3 miles, or a full 4 miles for the whole loop.

DIRECTIONS: From Highway 101 in Morgan Hill, exit on Bailey Avenue and travel west to

Santa Teresa Boulevard. Turn left and drive to Palm Avenue. Turn right and continue to avenue's end at the paved parking lot for Coyote Valley Open Space Preserve. A restroom and picnic area are nearby.

THE HIKE: From the trailhead join an old ranch road (Heart's Delight Trail) and hike along the valley floor along the base of a hill. Bear right when the trail splits and join Arrowhead Loop Trail. The path ascends gradually and at some length to picnic tables and an overlook. Enjoy grand vistas of Coyote Valley and well beyond.

Continue your ascent, cross two bridges and reach a second overlook. The path leads to a service road and to a short path extending to an isolated picnic table. You might think this hike saves the best for last as you descend sweeping grasslands back to the valley floor. Rejoin Heart's Delight Trail and return to the trailhead.

Moo-ve over: Cows share the trail with hikers in Coyote Valley.

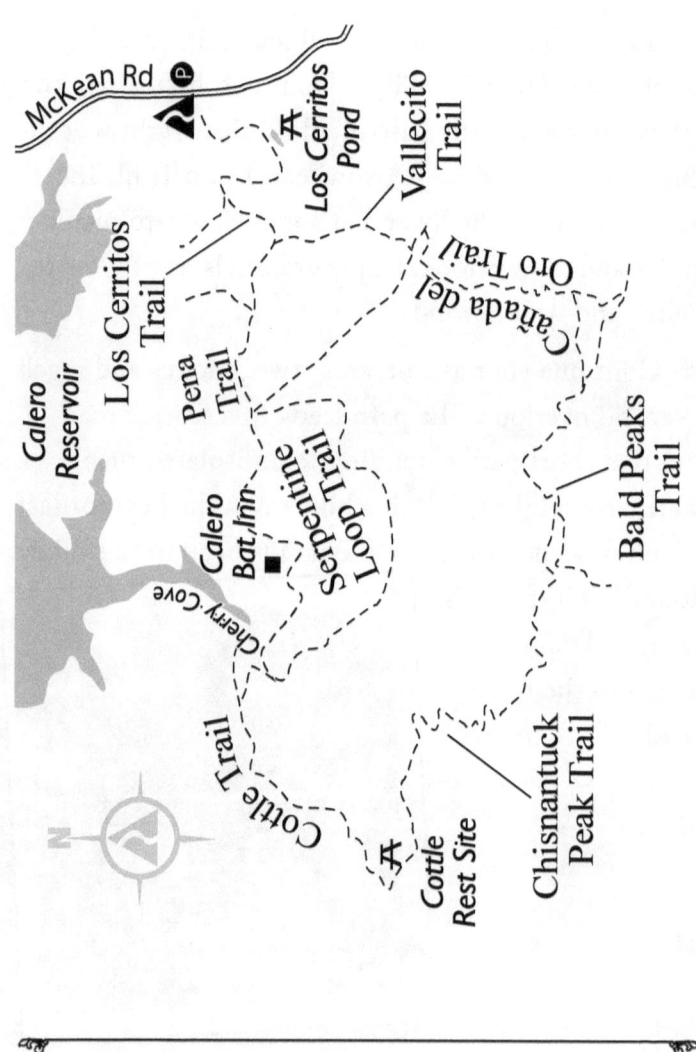

CALERO COUNTY PARK

LOS CERRITOS, SERPENTINE, COTTLE, BALD PEAKS TRAILS

8.2 miles round trip with 1,000-foot elevation gain

Boat, fish, hike. These are the fun activities awaiting you at Calero County Park located in the southernmost reaches of the South Bay.

Ride, too, if you bring your horse. Calero is very horse-friendly with water troughs and an equestrian-oriented staging area.

With 4,455 acres, Calero offers plenty of room to roam and a splendid feeling of isolation not found at other county parks located closer to suburbs. When you look out at the surrounding hills from the park's ridgetop trails, you see farms and ranches and hills without houses. About the only intrusion into the tranquil scene is the sound of boat engines reverberating off the lake and into the hills.

The boat launch is located on the north side of Calero Reservoir; the trail system spreads out from the south side. Choose from a variety of trails and terrain: creekside rambles, walks across meadows, up-and-down treks along the ridgelines.

Fashion a loop to fit your needs, beginning with easy jaunts on Los Cerritos Trail and Serpentine Loop Trail.

One of the longer loops is a seven-trail extravaganza that samples most of the park's natural attractions and tours the Bald Peaks area. You can shorten—or add to—the loop with additional trails.

DIRECTIONS: From Highway 101 in Morgan Hill, exit on Bailey Avenue and drive 3 miles southwest to McKenna Road. Turn left and proceed 0.6 mile to the large dirt parking lot for Calero County Park. The trailhead is located across the road.

Los Cerritos Pond, a peaceful part of Calero Park.

THE HIKE: Begin on the one trail (dirt road). At 0.2 mile, pass a left fork with Figueroa Trail and ascend a short distance to Los Cerritos Pond. Follow Los Cerritos trail to meet Pena Trail and continue your westward course.

At a 3-way junction join the north leg of Serpentine Loop Trail and about 2 miles out, reach the curious two-story Calero Bat Inn, a bat habitat on stilts. ("We'll leave the lights *off* for you," is the inn's amusing slogan.)

Hike near the reservoir, pass a junction with Cherry Cove Trail and descend to Cottle Trail, which bends south as it ascends a wooded ridge. After a mile, the trail delivers you to a meadow and "Cottle Rest Site" at the locale of an old homestead.

The ranch road ends and you continue on a footpath—Chisnantuck Trail—into thick woods. Climb in earnest and finally reach a bench with great vistas. A bit beyond the bench the path ends, and you embark on a dirt road (Bald Hills Peaks Trail), which travels up and down with the ridgeline for 1.7 miles—the best part of the hike.

Meet Canada del Oro Trail, a footpath for a time, then a dirt road. Join Figueroa Trail, then Vallecito Trail, which offers a pleasant 0.5 mile traverse across a grassy meadow back to Pena Trail. Retrace your steps back to the trailhead.

Monte Bello, one of the lovely, hiker-friendly Midpeninsula Open Space Preserves.

EVERY TRAIL TELLS A STORY.

II
Peninsula Parks & Preserves

HIKE ON.

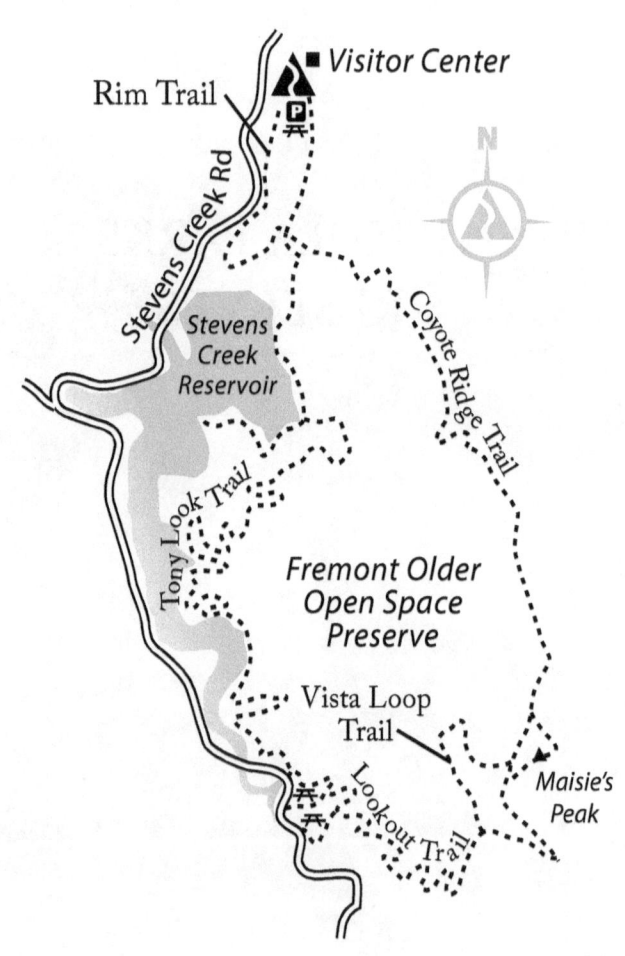

STEVENS CREEK COUNTY PARK
Tony Look, Coyote Ridge Trail

To Picnic Areas is 5.4 miles round trip with 200-foot elevation gain; return via Coyote Ridge is 6.2 miles with 600-foot gain

Tony Look Trail offers a mellow exploration of Stevens Creek County Park, which opened in 1924, Santa Clara County's very first park. Easy on the eye and easy to hike, a favorite length of the trail extends along the east side of Stevens Creek Reservoir and connects to higher and drier trails to make a loop in adjacent Fremont Older Open Space Preserve.

Before hitting the trail, let us honor its namesake, Claude "Tony" Look, accomplished conservationist and one of the all time great advocates for trails. Look was a founder and executive director of the Sempervirens Fund to protect redwoods. He founded the Santa Cruz Trails Association and began its annual Trails Day in 1969. The event went statewide, and led to the first National Trails Day in 1992.

Santa Clara County Parks Department dedicated a length of Stevens Creek Trail for Tony Look in 2001.

The county park's 1,063 acres surrounds Stevens Creek Reservoir, created in 1935 when a dam was built across Stevens Creek. (BTW, let's not confuse this reservoir-centered park with *Upper* Stevens Creek County Park, located to the southwest and so named because of its higher elevation.)

While Tony Look Trail is mostly shaded, Coyote Ridge is mostly an open slope—and not the trail to travel on a hot day! The paths linked together form a popular fitness loop hike that offers a bit of scenic variety, views and just enough hill climbing for a good cardio workout.

DIRECTIONS: From I-280 in Cupertino, take the Foothill Expressway exit, merge onto Foothill Boulevard and drive 1 mile south. Continue on Stevens Canyon Road 2 miles to the entrance of Stevens Creek County Park. You'll need to pay an entry fee (credit cards only). Continue past the visitor center to a picnic area and parking.

THE HIKE: Walk back up the road toward the visitor center and join signed Stevens Creek/Tony Look Trail. In its early going, it's a broad multi-use path that leads south toward the dam and spillway.

About 0.4 mile from the trailhead, reach a junction with Coyote Ridge Trail (a return option if you so choose). Continue south on Tony Look Trail, a footpath now, as it edges toward the reservoir, then bends away.

Switchbacks lead up brushy slopes with vistas out over the reservoir to the wooded west shore. Descend with more switchbacks over slopes sufficiently steep (and with a drop-off) that trail-builders felt compelled to add fencing along one section for hiker protection.

Tony Look Trail comes to an end close to Stevens Road and near a group of picnic areas. Return the way you came or hike on toward Coyote Ridge by joining 0.7-mile- long Lookout Trail near Madrone Picnic Area as it switchbacks steeply up wooded slopes into Fremont Older OSP.

At a junction with Vista Loop Trail, choose either leg (both lead to Coyote Ridge Trail), but I say take the right one because it serves up better vistas. Descend the wide dirt road and in 0.1 mile or so intersect signed Coyote Ridge Trail.

Turn left and soon note a side trail on your right that leads 0.2 mile to Maisie's Peak (1,180 feet), park high point. From the summit, enjoy views of the San Jose skyline, Moffett Air Field in Mountain View, and the hills of the East Bay. On particularly clear days, look for Mt. Diablo, San Francisco and Mt. Tamalpais.

Coyote Ridge Trail dips and rises, then for its final mile, descends steeply. (Keep a watchful eye out for mountain bikes zooming downhill.) When you intersect Tony Look Trail, retrace your steps back to the trailhead.

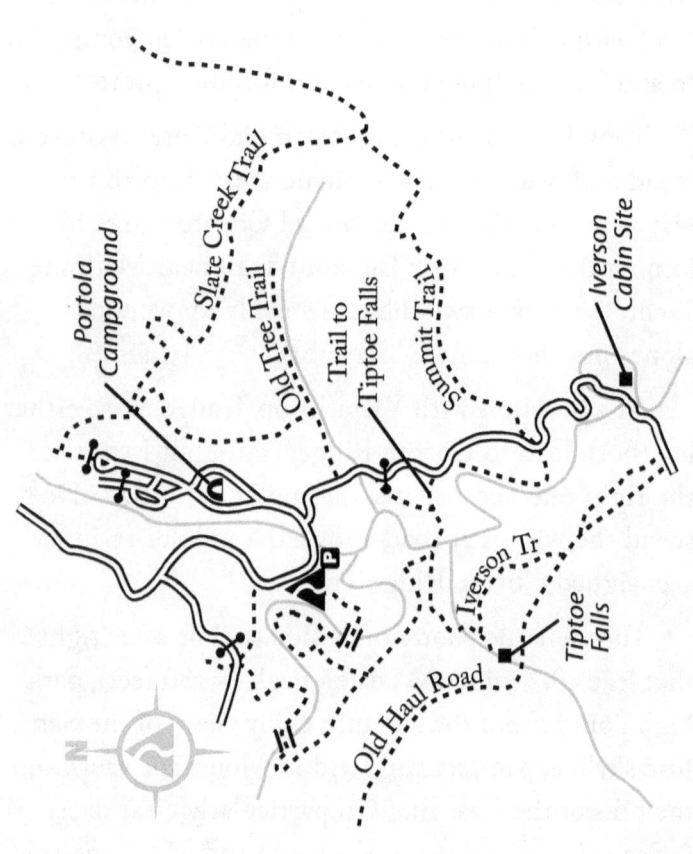

TheTrailmaster.com

Portola Redwoods State Park

Iverson, Summit, Slate Creek Trails

6 miles round trip; longer and shorter options possible

You could call this tranquil park, perched on the opposite side of the Santa Cruz Mountains from Big Basin Redwoods State Park, "Little Basin Redwoods State Park." Like its well-known cousin, Portola Redwoods State Park is a natural basin forested with coast redwoods.

Places like Portola still evoke the feeling of wild California. This wild feeling begins outside the park boundaries as you travel Alpine Road—an enjoyable drive.

Rangers refer to Portola as a "neighborhood park," meaning thus far, it's mostly locals who have discovered the hiking opportunities in this small redwood forest. The park centers around two creeks—Peters and Pescadero—that meander through a basin. Douglas fir and oaks cloak the ridges while redwoods, accompanied by huckleberry and ferns, cluster in cooler bottomlands.

Most redwoods in the area are second-growth trees. However, most "logging" at Portola was for shingle production; trees needed a very straight grain and were selectively cut. Many large trees escaped the ax and may be seen today inside the park, particularly along Peters Creek and Slate Creek.

One of my favorite day hikes in this park is a six-mile "walkabout" that utilizes five different trails. Drop in at the park visitor center to view the nature and history exhibits.

DIRECTIONS: From Interstate 280 (Junipero Serra Freeway), about six miles north of San Jose, exit on Saratoga Avenue and head south, joining Highway 9 in the town of Saratoga. Highway 9 ascends west into the mountains to a junction with Skyline Boulevard (Highway 35). Turn right (northwest) on Skyline and follow it to a junction with Alpine Road and the signed turnoff to Portola Redwoods State Park. Turn onto Alpine Road. After 3.5 miles, turn left on Portola State Park Road and continue 3 more miles to the park. Look for parking near the visitor center.

THE HIKE: Join Sequoia Nature Trail, which begins behind the park visitor center. Tramp through the redwood forest, cross Pescadero Creek, and loop around Louise Austin Wilson Grove, site of the Shell Tree.

Next join Iverson Trail, which meanders along Pescadero Creek. A short side trail leads to diminutive, fern-framed Tip-Toe Falls.

Iverson Trail visits the ruins of Iverson Cabin as it meets a park service road. A right leads to Old Haul Road which in turn leads five miles to San Mateo Memorial County Park. You turn left, cross Pescadero Creek on a bridge, and soon arrive at a signed junction with Summit Trail.

True to its name, Summit Trail ascends some 600 feet in elevation to a rather undistinguished summit. It then dips briefly to a saddle and a signed junction with Slate Creek Trail. It's another mile east to the park's trail camp, a pleasant, though waterless, rest stop.

From the saddle, Slate Creek Trail descends a pleasant mile west, then contours south to Old Tree Trail and the park's campground. Walk through the campground, then join the park road for a brief walk back to the park visitor center.

Pretty little fern-framed Tip-Toe Falls.

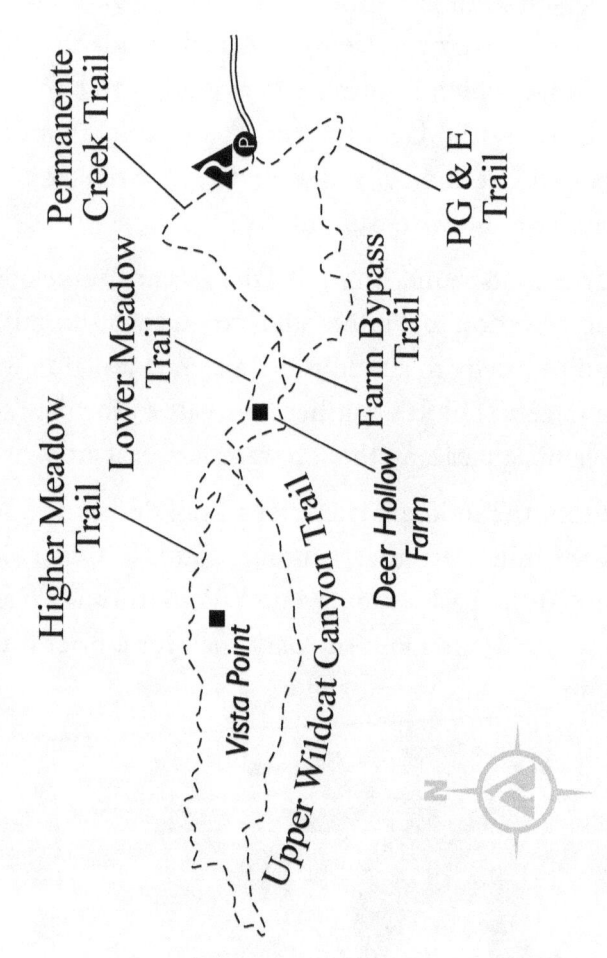

Rancho San Antonio

Lower Meadow, High Meadow, Upper Wildcat Canyon Trails

5.5 mile loop with 700-foot elevation gain

With about a half-million visitors a year, Rancho San Antonio sure is a popular (some would say crowded) park. Easy to access from many Santa Clara County locales, the park attracts scores of runners from casual joggers to ultra-fit long-distance marathoners. (Runner's World magazine was founded and headquartered in Mountain View; during the 1980s, many world-class runners frequented these trails.) A steady stream of families follow the well-beaten path from the picnic areas and tennis courts to Deer Hollow (a model farm), and the park attracts an array of hikers of all ages and abilities.

However, before you scratch Rancho San Antonio off your "To Hike" list, know that it's a pretty big park (nearly 4,000 acres) with 24 miles of trail that lead through the woods and across high meadows for far-reaching vistas of the South Bay.

If this is your first visit to Rancho San Antonio (and if you're hiking with kids), you must begin with the easy 1.1-mile walk to Deer Hollow Farm, a working farm with an organic garden, restored late 19th-century ranch buildings, and all the basic domestic animals—chickens, pigs, cows, sheep, goats.

From Deer Hollow Farm (well-named, deer are numerous in the park), hikers have access to many well-signed trails. Challenging PG&E Trail and Upper Meadow Trail add up to a rigorous 9-mile loop. Hardest hike in the park is the ascent of Black Mountain, a 16-mile trip trek with 2,400-foot elevation gain. One of my favorites is a moderately easy loop via High Meadow Trail and Wildcat Canyon Trail.

DIRECTIONS: From I-280 in Cupertino, take the Foothill Expressway exit and head briefly south on Foothill Boulevard. Turn right on Cristo Rey Drive and drive a mile to Rancho San Antonio County Park (operated by the Midpeninsula Regional Open Space District). Continue to the last lot at the end of the park road.

THE HIKE: Follow the paved trail over a bridge and join the path leading to Deer Hollow Farm. After 0.25 mile, reach the boundary with Rancho San Antonio Open Space Preserve. Walk the paved road (all the way to the farm) or opt for adjacent dirt Lower Meadow Trail that rejoins the road at the 0.8-mile-mark.

Just past the farm, turn left, continue past Farm Bypass Trail and porta-potties, and turn right on signed High Meadow Trail. Begin a stiff ascent via switchbacks amidst oaks and over slopes seasonally splashed with wildflowers. A bench offers a rest stop, and views expand to include the park's gentle hills and bold Black Mountain. Just short of two miles out, the trail crests and passes a junction with Wildcat Loop Trail and at 2.5 miles meets Upper High Meadow Trail (a fine 2-mile addition to the hike).

Go left on Upper Wildcat Canyon Trail and descend brushy slopes to the cool canyon floor shaded by California bay, madrone, and maple. Make a gentle descent, crisscrossing the creek several times over footbridges. Continue meandering along the shady creek to trail's end and a meet-up with High Meadow Trail near Deer Hollow Farm and retrace your steps back to the trailhead.

Yes, deer. Be on the lookout for them in the hills and meadows.

Monte Bello

Stevens Creek, Indian Creek, Bella Vista Trails

6-mile loop with 700-foot elevation gain

Monte Bello, "the beautiful mountain" in Italian, is just that—a handsome 2,700-foot high ridge, cut by creeks, greened with grass, cloaked with oak woodlands and fir forests. It's a spirit-uplifting place for hikers, and no doubt an inspiring backdrop for residents of Palo Alto, Los Altos and Cupertino.

The preserve's featured pathway is Stevens Creek Nature Trail, which tours a variety of landscapes from grassland to chaparral to evergreen forests. A close-up view of the San Andreas Fault Zone is particularly illuminating. Fault movement has produced two different soil systems and thus two different communities: woodland on one side, brush and grass on the other.

Stevens Creek Nature Trail also explores other evidence of fault action in the form of a cattail-lined sag pond. Interpretive signs examine ladybugs, Douglas fir and California's official state rock—bluish-gray serpentine.

The preserve also offers longer trails that probe upper Stevens Creek Canyon and ascend Monte Bello's high ridge. Canyon Trail (7.6 miles one way) connects Monte Bello with Saratoga Gap.

After exploring Stevens Creek and the San Andreas Fault, this hike climbs, and then travels along, Monte Bello Ridge to its highest point, Black Mountain. Reward for the ascent is a great panoramic view of the Santa Clara Valley, Santa Cruz Mountains and much more.

DIRECTIONS: From I-280 in Los Altos Hills, exit on Page Mill Road/Arastadero Road. Drive south on Page Mill Road 7 miles to the parking area and trailhead on the left.

THE HIKE: Join Stevens Creek Nature Trail (a footpath) and switchback down to mixed woodland of oaks, bay and madrone. Cross a tributary of Stevens Creek on a bridge, and descend wooden steps to Stevens Creek. Cross the creek (can be impassable in times of very high water).

Ascend to meet Skid Road Trail (a dirt road) and bear left on this onetime logging road. Cross Stevens Creek two more times on bridges. Climb more steeply to junction Canyon Trail (a dirt road). Bear right and begin a rigorous ascent. Two miles out, Canyon

Trail goes right and you bear left onto Indian Creek Trail (a dirt road) and ascend Monte Bello Ridge.

Pass a side trail that leads to Black Mountain Trail Camp, a rare overnight spot for backpackers in these parts. Head for the top of Black Mountain by continuing with Indian Creek Trail to meet Monte Bello Road, turn right and ascend to Black Mountain. Enjoy eye-popping vistas from San Jose to San Francisco Bay to Mt. Diablo. Wow!

Return to the turnoff for the trail camp, walk through the camp, and reach a four-way trail intersection. Join narrow Old Ranch Trail, which angles leftward, makes a mellow descent, and delivers great views. At yet another junction, merge onto Bella Vista Trail, which leads to a marshy area and a sag pond. Meet the eastern leg of Stevens Nature Trail and loop back to the trailhead.

Monte Bello: Ascend the "beautiful mountain" through oak woodland and fir forest for fine views.

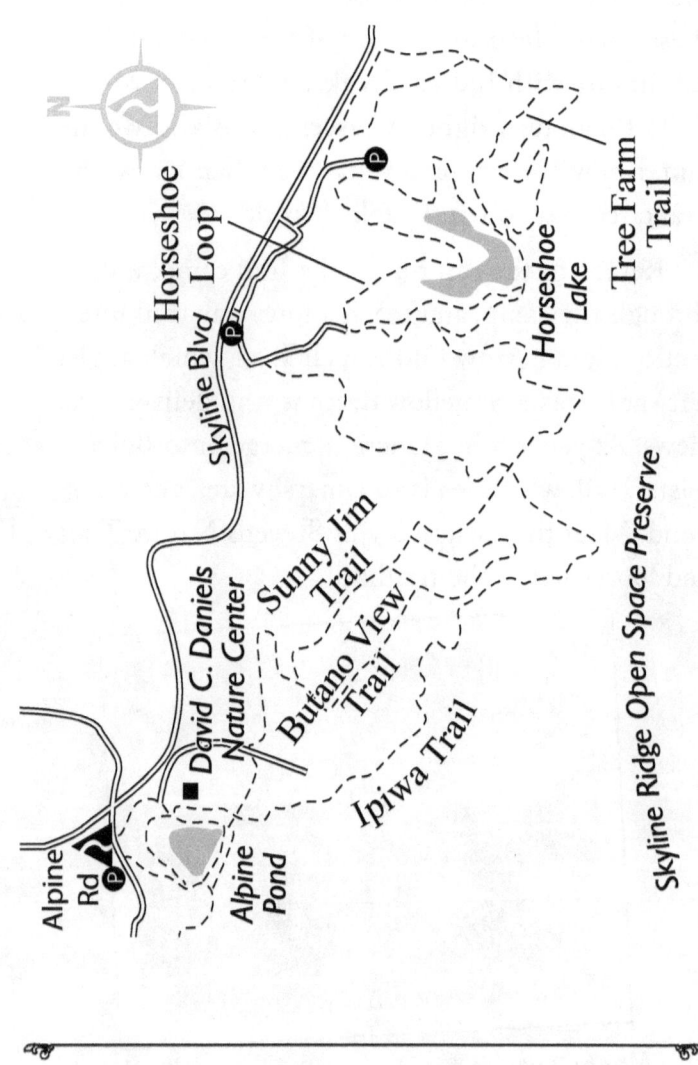

Skyline Ridge

Ipiwa, Alpine Pond Loop, Horseshoe Loop Trails

From Russian Ridge OSP parking lot to Horseshoe Lake is 4 miles round trip

Perched atop Skyline Ridge, this preserve beckons hikers with two sweet little ponds and a path that connects them.

Alpine Pond is a favorite with wildlife watchers, especially with kids, who like seeing all the pond dwellers—crayfish, western pond turtles, newts and frogs, plus lots of birds including coots, cormorants, scrub jays and red-winged blackbirds. Stop by the David C. Daniels Nature Center (open on the weekends, April through November) to learn more.

Horseshoe Lake is also a good place to spot native and migratory birds and offers an overlook with picnic tables under the shade of oaks. Alpine Pond and Horseshoe Lake were created in the 1950s to supply water for a hog ranch and other agricultural uses. Both ponds have loop trails that circle them, and are wheelchair- and stroller-friendly.

Before the Midpeninsula Open Space District purchased the land in 1982, it was used as Christmas tree farm and hog ranch. One owner was the colorful politician James "Sunny Jim" Rolph, who was mayor of San Francisco from 1912 to 1931, and later served a term as governor.

The path that connects the ponds, Ipiwa Trail (also part of the Bay Area Ridge Trail), travels along a ridge cloaked in chaparral and grasslands. It serves up fabulous views over the Santa Cruz Mountains. Now a little bad news: While the first half of the hike to a viewpoint is near-perfect, the second half is very much in earshot of the roar of traffic on Skyline Boulevard, not to mention a nearby firing range.

This hike begins at the park nature center and uses the Russian Ridge OSP Trailhead.

DIRECTIONS: From I-280 in Los Altos, exit on Page Mill Road and drive 9 miles west to Skyline Boulevard (35). Continue across Skyline onto Alpine Road and turn right into the Russian Ridge OSP parking lot. (Reach Skyline Ridge Preserve's main entrance by driving one mile south on Skyline Boulevard.)

THE HIKE: From the parking lot, walk through the tunnel beneath Alpine Road and emerge near the Daniels Nature Center. A pleasant 0.5-mile long trail, accessible to all ages and abilities, loops around the center.

Left of the nature center, join Ipiwa Trail, which meanders through oak woodland, and open grassland for eye-popping vistas. After one mile, reach a junction with Sunny Jim Trail (dirt road), turn right, and continue onto the Horseshoe Loop Trail to explore the picturesque eastern side of the lake.

Alternatively, hike counterclockwise around Horseshoe Lake (1.1 miles) and rest/have lunch at the picnic tables overlooking the lake before you head back to the trailhead.

A path between two ponds in Skyline Ridge Preserve.

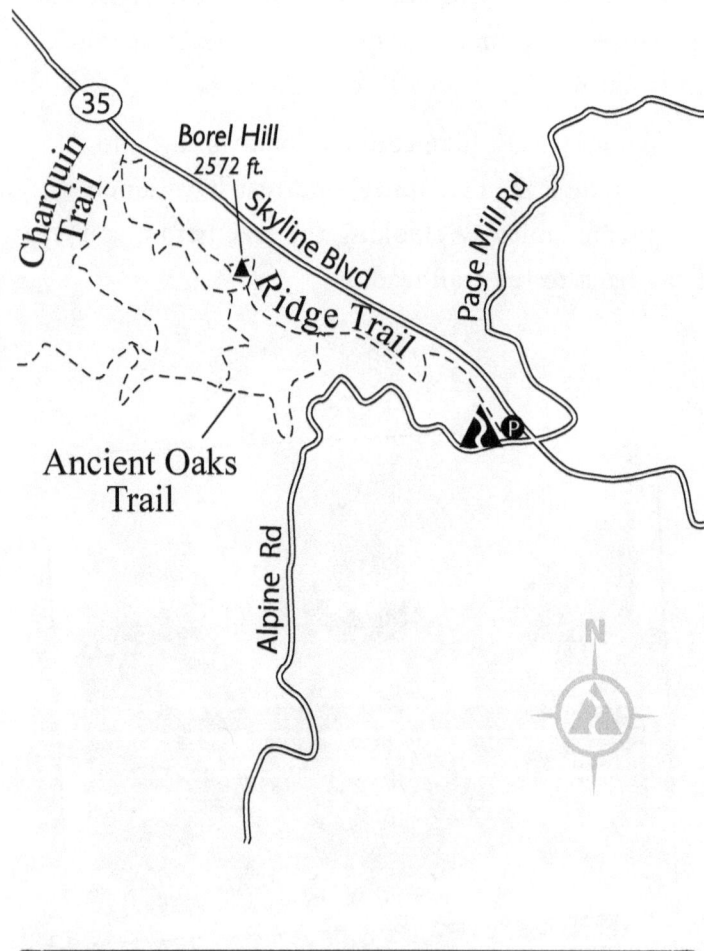

Russian Ridge

Ridge, Ancient Oaks, Charquin Trails

3.5 miles round trip with 300-foot elevation gain

"Ten miles from I-280 and a world apart." That's one way to describe Russian Ridge Open Space Preserve, a top Bay Area locale to enjoy wildflower displays. From April to early May is usually the peak time to check out the prodigious bursts of blossom—fields of lupine and poppies, plus cream cups, owl's clover, mule's ear...

Well, you get the idea.

The preserve's topography favors this kind of wildflower show. Unlike more typical misty and damp redwood-filled parks in the Santa Cruz Mountains, Russian Ridge features a rather unusual open and treeless ridge. Along with fostering fabulous wildflower displays, the ridge also offers spectacular, clear-day vistas of the Bay Area and San Mateo County coastline.

Even when the flower show is over, Russian Ridge offers great hiking: warm (but not too hot) summers, autumn with clear, crisp days and great views.

Russian Ridge, named for a Russian immigrant who grazed cattle and owned a dairy farm here from 1920 to 1950, was saved from subdivision in the late 1970s and in the 1980s became a preserve.

Speaking of cows, some still remain, grazing the slopes of Mindego Hill. Check out the new trail that leads to the top of the hill. Stop by the trailhead on Alpine Road and meander the paved pathway to a vista point.

This hike is a sampler of the preserve, an engaging loop that serves up great views of San Francisco Bay and Ancient Oaks Trail that meanders amidst antiquarian oaks. For a superb short ramble along Russian Ridge, take the 1.4-mile round trip hike to Borel Hill (2,572 feet) for fabulous panoramic vistas of the South Bay.

DIRECTIONS: From I-280 in Los Altos, exit on Page Mill Road and drive 9 miles west to Skyline Boulevard (35). Continue across Skyline onto Alpine Road and turn right into the Russian Ridge OSP parking lot. (Additional parking at Caltrans Vista Point opposite preserve gate.)

THE HIKE: Join signed Ridge Trail, which leads along the grassy ridge parallel to Skyline Boulevard.

At 0.5 mile, reach a junction with Ancient Oaks Trail and go left, south across grasslands and visiting groves of wondrous and picturesque coast live oak. About 1.5 mile from the trailhead, Ancient Oaks Trail ends at a 3-way junction.

Bear right on Charquin Trail and climb moderately to a junction just short of a trailhead/parking area on Skyline Boulevard. Bear right on Bay Area Ridge Trail, noting that there is an additional "Ridge Trail" that leads closer to Skyline; the paths reconnect in 0.5 mile.)

Continue on the grassy slopes seasonally sprinkled with wildflowers and along the backbone of the ridge to what is usually the epicenter of the annual flower show. Later in the spring the slopes are overwhelmed by tall green grass that turns brown in summer, gold in autumn.

Ridge Trail makes a mellow descent, offers views of neighboring Skyline Ridge and Monte Bello preserves, and returns to a junction with Ancient Oaks Trail. Retrace your steps 0.5 mile back to the trailhead.

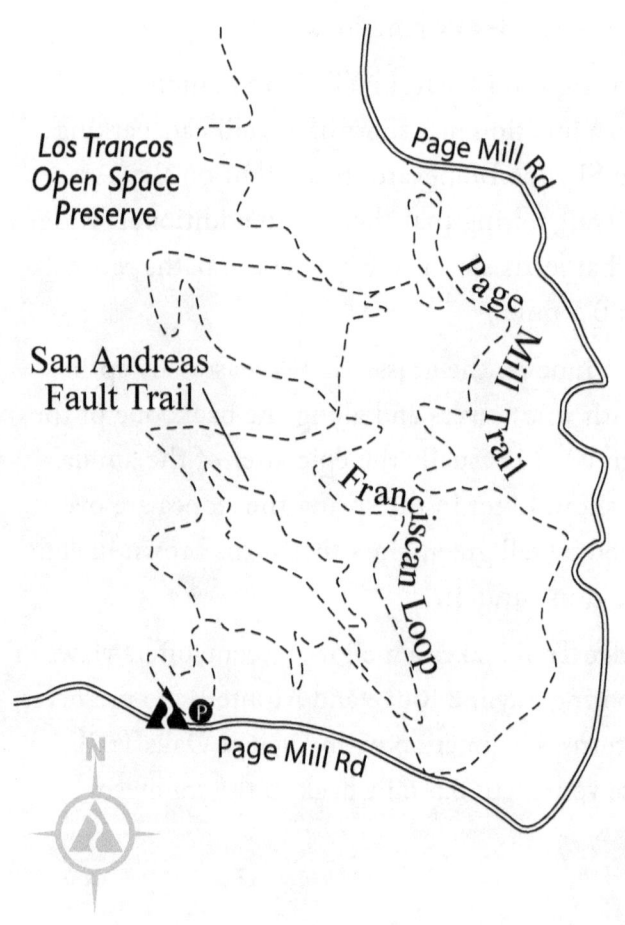

LOS TRANCOS

SAN ANDREAS FAULT, FRANCISCAN LOOP, LOST CREEK LOOP TRAILS

San Andreas Fault Trail is 1.5 miles round trip; loop via Franciscan and Lost Creek Trails is 3 miles round trip with 300-foot elevation gain.

My first hikes in the earthquake zone were motivated by a kind of perverse fatalism, but after a while I began to enjoy the sheer beauty of the San Andreas Fault: the crushed and uplifted rocks, the jagged streambeds and the long gashes through the sweeping grasslands.

That's why I like to hike Los Trancos Open Space Preserve, which offers attractive trails and close-up views of the fault zone. San Andreas Fault Trail is an interpretive path that offers the hiker a strange beauty, as well as an introduction to a world of scarps and sag ponds, tectonic plates and continental drift.

Supplementing this fascinating trail are the Franciscan Loop Trail and Lost Creek Loop Trail, which offer the hiker the opportunity for longer explorations of the preserve. Highlights along these loops are fern-lined Los Trancos Creek and antiquarian oaks that lost large limbs during the 1906 San Francisco Earthquake.

We Californians live on a landmass called the Pacific Plate, which like other continental plates is drifting on the surface of the globe. Our northbound Pacific Plate meets the North American Plate at the San Andreas Fault. The two plates creep along past each other ever-so-slowly. Friction locks our plate with that of North America at certain points near San Francisco and Los Angeles, but that doesn't prevent the plates from moving. Stress builds up, energy is released and whammo! We have earthquakes. Something to think about on the San Andreas Fault Trail.

DIRECTIONS: From Interstate 280 in Los Altos Hills, exit on Page Mill Road and wind 7.2 miles west (just past the parking area for Monte Bello Open Space Preserve on the left) to Los Trancos Open Space Preserve and a parking area on the right. The preserve is located 1.5 miles east of Skyline Boulevard.

THE HIKE: Join signed San Andreas Fault Trail, which soon leads to a vista point and Stop #1 of the 9-stop tour. Continue to Stop #2 and more views—north to San Francisco and far east to Mt. Diablo. Press on past a junction with Franciscan

Loop Trail and follow the numbers. Stop #4 is the marquee attraction—a fence that moved 3 feet during the great quake of 1906.

After Stop #9, head back to the junction with Franciscan Loop Trail and go left. Cross a meadow and meander along the creek, crossing a dike over the sluggish watercourse. Descend amidst blackberry bushes and other lush vegetation and meet Lost Creek Loop Trail at about the 1.5-mile mark. Bear right on the narrow path, crossing a boardwalk over a boggy area and making a 0.9-mile long loop, descending to Los Trancos Creek, then climbing again.

Back at the junction with Franciscan Loop Trail, go right and hike 0.6 mile back to the trailhead.

A highlight of San Andreas Fault Trail: This fence moved three feet during the 1906 San Francisco Earthquake.

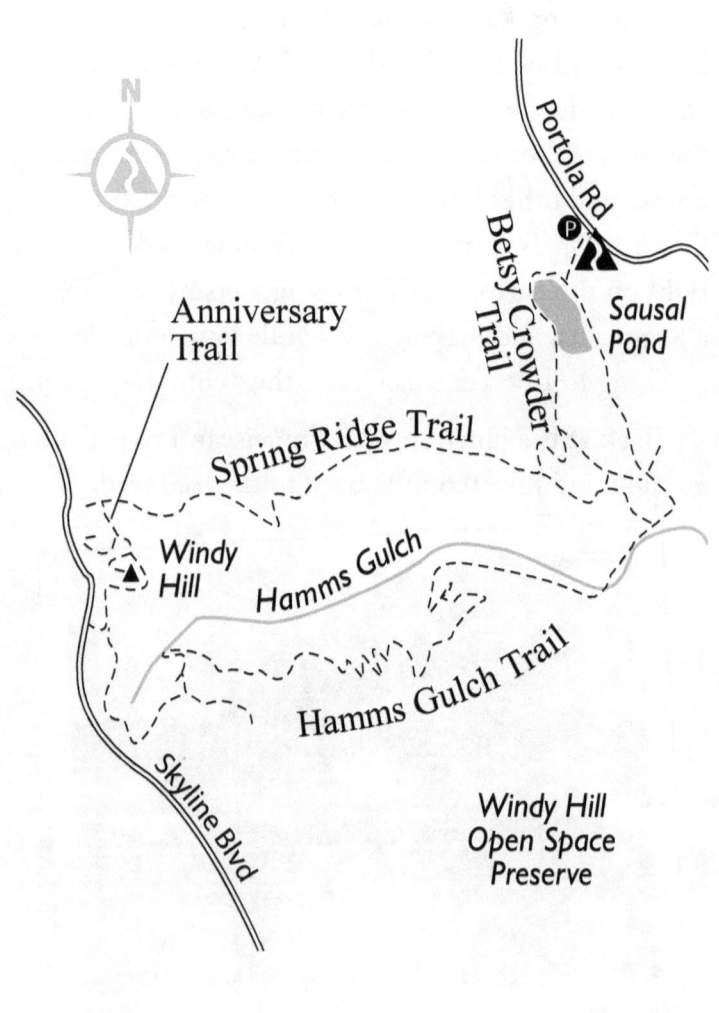

WINDY HILL

HAMMS GULCH, SPRING RIDGE, BETSY CROWDER TRAILS

7.6 miles round trip with 1,400-foot elevation gain

Windy this hill may be, but it's the memorable views from this two-knobbed promontory that linger in a hiker's memory. Summit views include a 360-degree panorama of bay and ocean, mountains and metropolis. The wind is a natural white noise, too, and covers the sound of modern transport—trains, planes and automobiles, not to mention trucks and helicopters.

The preserve's grassy slopes, which extend from Portola Valley up to Skyline Boulevard, as well as its canyons and steep ridges, are crossed by good trails that offer fine loop possibilities. A trailhead on Skyline lets you start the hike with a descent. If you just want to hike out for a view from the top of Windy Hill, this is the best way to go.

You have two choices from the Portola trailhead: Ascend via a very steep fire road along Spring Ridge or by way of woodsy Hamms Gulch with assistance from well-crafted switchbacks. I thought everybody would want to ascend via Hamms Gulch but on my last visit a majority of hikers were doing the reverse. Go figure.

DIRECTIONS: From I-280 in Portola Valley, exit on Alpine Road, head west 3 miles, and turn right onto Portola Road. Drive 1 mile and turn left into the Windy Hill OSP.

THE HIKE: Begin with a short path that meets Spring Ridge Trail at a junction by Sausal Pond. Go left and hike along the preserve boundary near Alpine Road. Meander a mixed woodland of oaks, madrone, and maples past a junction at the 0.6- mile mark with Sequoia Trail, and continue 0.2 mile to another junction. Cross a private drive and continue straight onto Hamms Gulch Trail, which drops to a creek then begins to climb.

Picturesque oaks predominate in the lower reaches of Hamms Gulch and, farther along, tall Douglas fir join the eclectic mix of trees. Most of the ascent is aided by well-done switchbacks, and benches offer rest along the way.

At about the hike's halfway point, Hamms Gulch Trail junctions Lost Trail, and you go right, emerging from the woods onto more level ground. Take a break at a picnic area/trailhead by Skyline Boulevard. The wind may increase and the clouds zoom by as you embark on Anniversary Trail, which leads to an official overlook, and to the 1,905-foot summit of Windy Hill.

Enjoy 360-degree views from the two high points, then descend to a junction near Skyline where you turn right on Spring Ridge Trail, a fire road. Begin a steep, knee-jarring descent through oak-dotted grassland. On good wildflower years, open areas can be carpeted with lupine. The trail drops through mixed woods and pops out occasionally for vistas of Silicon Valley.

Meet Betsy Crowder Trail at the 6.8-mile mark and go left on the path that honors the dedicated conservationist and trail guide writer. The trail crosses a meadow, descends through woodland near Sausal Pond, and leads back to the short connector trail and trailhead.

Windy Hill: Two windy high points offer panoramic views.

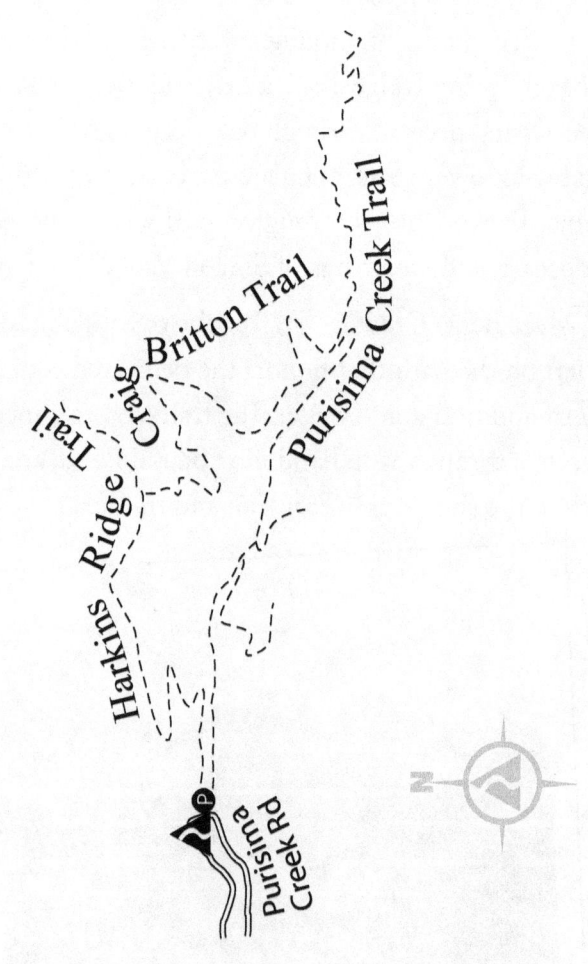

PURISIMA CREEK REDWOODS

PURISIMA CREEK, CRAIG BRITTON, HARKINS RIDGE TRAIL

Loop via Purisima Creek and Harkins Ridge is 7.4 miles round trip with 1,100-foot elevation gain

Perched on the crest of the Santa Cruz Mountains, the redwoods above Half Moon Bay beckon the hiker with enchanting forest trails and, when the foggy curtain parts, glorious coastal and mountain views. More than 20 miles of trail weave through the redwoods and a mixed forest of Douglas fir, tan oak and madrone in 4,711-acre Purisima Creek Redwoods Open Space Preserve.

Park centerpiece is year-round Purisima Creek which, joined by smaller streams, tumbles from Skyline Ridge and flows three miles through the preserve. Tall, second-growth redwoods line the creek and adjoining steep-sided canyon.

The redwoods, accompanied by ferns, blackberry bushes and many flowering plants, are the northernmost groves in the Santa Cruz Mountains. Like the redwoods, the preserve's main trail sticks close to Purisima Creek.

Loggers of the 1850s and later, found the trees were just too big to haul up the steep canyon walls and the fate of most of Purisima Creek's first-growth redwoods was to be cut into shingles. It took more than 50 years (to the early 1900s) before all the redwoods were logged.

Purisima Creek Trail is a wide, flat trail shaded by redwoods. Craig Britton Trail extends from the bottom of Purisima Canyon to the top of Harkins Ridge. Then it's a steep descent along the ridge with great vistas along the way.

DIRECTIONS: From its junction with Highway 92 in Half Moon Bay, travel south on Highway 1 about 4.3 miles. Turn left on Verde Road and after 0.25 mile continue straight at a split in the road onto Purisima Creek Road. Drive 3.7 miles to Purisima Creek Redwoods OSP and parking.

THE HIKE: Purisima Creek Trail leads along the south side of the creek. Admiring the second-growth redwoods, ascend moderately.

At 1.3 miles, cross a bridge and pass a junction with Grabtown Gulch Trail. (This trail ascends very steeply into a ferny gulch, climbs through a mixed forest of tanoak, madrone, Douglas fir and young redwoods and you can make a loop along the preserve's south boundary near Tunitas Creek Road.)

Climb moderately amidst ferns, towering redwoods, and magnificent maples to intersect signed Craig Britton Trail, 2.3 miles from the trailhead. Join this lovely footpath on a moderate ascent through a lush redwood forest. The path crosses Soda Creek on a little bridge, angles west, then north, then southwest, leaves the redwoods at the 4-mile mark, and enters a thick coastal scrub community.

Approaching the ridgetop, gain superb clear-day vistas of the northernmost Santa Cruz Mountains unfolding toward the Pacific and Half Moon Bay. After a bit more climbing, meet Harkins Ridge Trail (a dirt fire road) at the 5-mile mark and begin a steep descent. Enjoy views framed by ceanothus and madrone for another mile or so before the trail angles toward Purisima Creek and plunges through the redwood forest back to the trailhead.

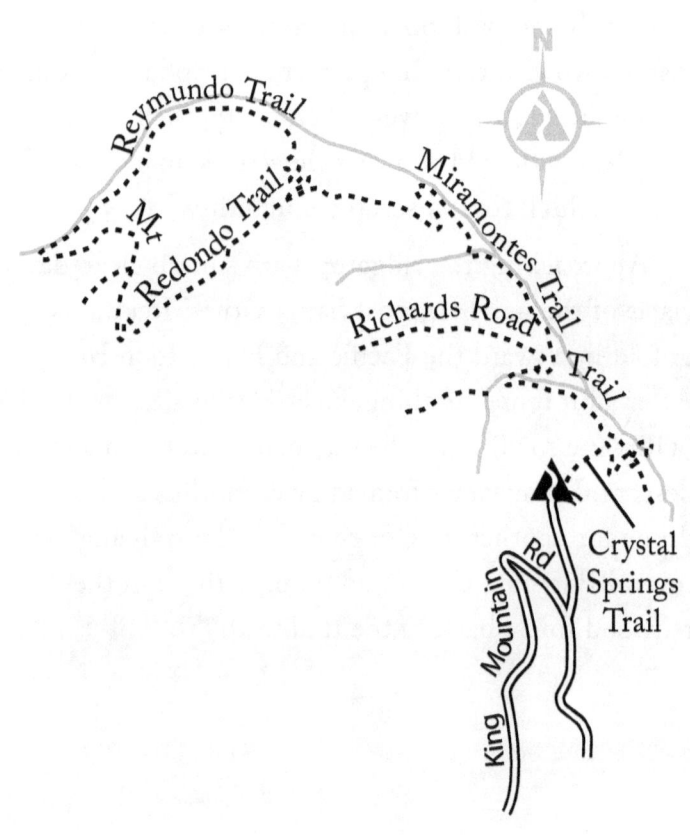

PHLEGER ESTATE

CRYSTAL SPRING, RICHARDS ROAD, MIRAMONTE TRAILS

From Huddart County Park to Phleger Estate is 4.2 miles round trip with 200-foot elevation gain; loop via Raymundo and Mt. Redondo Trails is 6.6 miles round trip with 600-foot gain

Woodsy Woodside, one of the Bay Area's priciest and most rustic residential areas, has a park that seems very much in keeping with its neighborhood. You half expect a gated entry or valet parking for the Phleger Estate.

Prominent San Francisco attorney Herman Phleger owned this land of steep canyons and second-growth redwoods at a time when property located 40 miles south of San Francisco was quite rural and removed from city life. Phleger managed to commute by auto over poor roads to offices in the city during the 1930s.

Phleger's 1,227-acre parcel became the southernmost unit of the Golden Gate National Recreation Area in 1995.

The only convenient hiking access to Phleger is by way of adjacent Huddart County Park. Deep and steep ravines, frequently wrapped in fog, support dense stands of redwood. Higher and drier slopes are cloaked in oaks. The estate's main trail traces West Union Creek, which just happens to lie directly on the San Andreas Fault.

DIRECTIONS: From Highway 280 in Woodside, take the Highway 84 (Woodside Road) exit and head west through Woodside for 1.7 miles to Kings Mountain Road. Turn right and travel 1.5 miles to Huddart County Park (entry fee). Park in the first lot, just past the entrance station.

THE HIKE: The wide path lined by a split-rail fence, winds through redwood and madrone as it skirts the Zwierlein Picnic Area. In 0.2 mile you'll join Crystal Spring Trail, sticking with this well-signed path as it passes several trail junctions, then junctions Richards Road. Bear left and a short 0.1 mile ascent up the dirt road will bring you to signed Miramonte Trail and entry to the Phleger Estate.

Join fern-lined Miramonte Trail as it travels alongside Union Creek. Watch for the abundant deer gamboling through the woods and a multitude of banana slugs slithering across the path. An impressive sign, topped by an iron Indian astride a horse, marks the dedication site of the Phleger Estate.

The path continues along bubbling Union Creek before abruptly and briefly turning south and ascending above the creek. Soon the trail changes direction again and heads west to a T-intersection with Mt. Redondo and Raymundo trails. Turn right on Raymundo Trail and begin a counter-clockwise tour of the mountain. Saunter along Union Creek for a bit, then climb above it to another junction marked with a sign and iron Indian.

Unless training for a trek to Nepal, ignore Lonely Trail, which ascends 1,000 feet in elevation to Skyline Boulevard. Instead, bid adieu to Raymundo Trail as it gives way to Mt. Redondo Trail and join this pleasant path as it dips to a trickling creek, crosses it, and descends back to the junction with Miramonte Trail. From this junction, retrace your steps back to the trailhead.

Trail signs here are works-of-art, complete with a Native American on horseback.

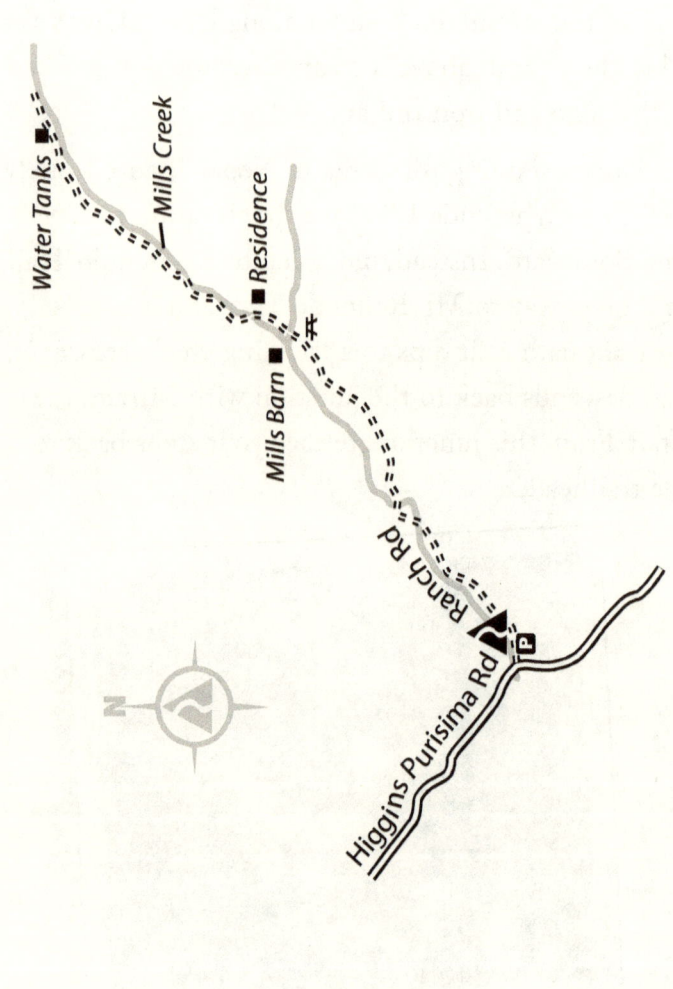

Burleigh Murray Ranch State Park

Burleigh Murray Ranch Trail

To old barn is 2 miles round trip with 100-foot elevation gain; to trail's end is 4 miles round trip

Burleigh Murray Ranch State Park is not your typical park in these parts. Rolling grassland, eucalyptus grove windbreaks, an old barn and a bunkhouse—this is ranch country, not the redwood country more typically associated with the Santa Cruz Mountains.

Beginning in the 1860s, the valley of Mill Creek and surrounding slopes were used for hay-growing and cattle grazing. The state purchased the land in 1983 and California State Parks has continued with the historical ranch theme with the park, and leaving the land almost completely undeveloped.

Burleigh Murray was born on the ranch in 1865; his father came to California from Vermont during the Gold Rush and started the dairy farm, located a few miles inland from Half Moon Bay in 1857.

In Burleigh Murray Ranch State Park, the prized historic structure is an old dairy barn, known as an English bank barn (because it's built into the hillside to facilitate loading from its upper heights); such barns are extremely rare in the U.S. Originally the barn was a very large one—200 feet long, with a 100-cow capacity.

Some handsome stonework, rusted farm machinery and a 1930s ranch house (now the park ranger's residence) adds to the rustic scene. The foundation of the barn, as well as an unreinforced arched stone bridge, were constructed with traditional Italian masonry methods that date back to Roman times. Photo opportunities are many on the old ranch.

Meandering through Burleigh Murray Ranch State Park is Mills Creek, named not for the considerable number of Santa Cruz Mountains sawmills, but rather for the Mills family, first owners of the ranch. The first mile of trail, a nearly flat, wide fire road (called "Ranch Road" on some maps), extends along Mill Creek to the old barn. Along the banks of the creek grows a tangle of ceanothus, nettle, blackberries, and plenty of poison oak. Extra-large eucalyptus rise high above the trail, which continues another mile past the old barn before ending unceremoniously in thickets of nettles and poison oak.

DIRECTIONS: From Highway 1, just south of the town of Half Moon Bay, turn east on Higgins-Purisima Road and immediately continue straight onto Purisima Canyon Road following it 1.5 miles to the small parking lot for Burleigh Murray Ranch

State Park on the north (left) side of the road, located a short distance from the entrance to the park.

THE HIKE: The flat, brush-lined road follows Mill Creek for a 0.5 mile before crossing, then re-crossing it via bridges. A mile out, the road passes a eucalyptus-shaded picnic site, angles left past the ranch house-turned-ranger's residence, crosses a bridge and brings you to the large dilapidated barn.

The route beyond the barn is an ever-narrowing footpath through Mill Creek Canyon. For decades the trail has had a rep for being poorly maintained. Beware of stinging nettle, blackberry brambles and poison oak. Whether overgrown or not the path continues through a narrow valley squeezed between steep brush-covered hills.

At 2 miles, it reaches a trio of leaky water tanks, then soon peters out in the thick coastal scrub.

They don't make 'em like they used to: a rare English bank barn

Sweeping beaches and dramatic coastal bluffs on the San Mateo County Coast.

EVERY TRAIL TELLS A STORY.

III

ON THE WATERFRONT

HIKE ON.

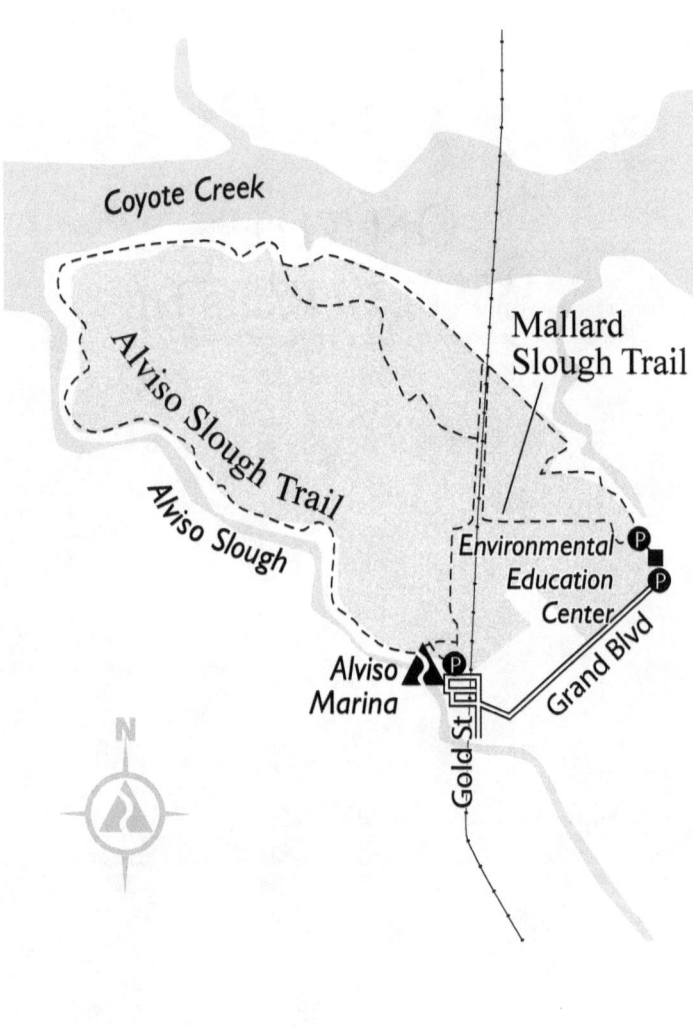

SAN FRANCISCO BAY NWR
Alviso Slough Trail

9-mile loop

It's surprising to say the least: In the midst of the nation's high tech industry lies a large and wildlife-friendly wetlands that attracts millions of migratory birds. TiVo Corporation headquarters is located only a mile as the Canada goose flies from Alviso Slough on the southernmost edge of San Francisco Bay.

The Alviso area of San Francisco Bay National Wildlife Refuge offers stellar bird-watching. More than 280 bird species have been counted at the refuge, a stopover on the Pacific Flyway. Look for ducks, mallards, cormorants and scores of California gulls. The birds are especially photogenic at sunset, in silhouette.

The little community of Alviso was all business back in the 1850s; it was San Jose's port and the valley's products—fruits, vegetables, lumber, mercury ore and more—were loaded onto steamships for transport to San Francisco and beyond.

Alas for Alviso, its days as a bustling port ended in 1864 when the San Jose-San Francisco rail line was completed.

Plan a post-hike visit to Alviso, said to be the Bay Area's low spot at 8 feet below sea level. Check out the historic Bayside Cannery (once the nation's third largest) and the quaint Victorian-era South Bay Yacht Club.

Cargill Salt Company's operation near Alviso is one of only two sea salt works in the U.S. A unique combination of soil composition, Mediterranean climate and, of course, plentiful seawater make the fringes of the South Bay perfect for salt-making. The Alviso salt evaporation ponds are a colorful sight because water color varies by seasons and salinity—blue, green, pumpkin and magenta. You'd think the ponds would be hostile to all life forms, but no, some 70 species of birds feed at the shallow (1.5-foot-deep) ponds, and they are breeding areas for the endangered California clapper rail.

Choose from a variety of breezy and easy trails. Marsh View Trail (0.4 mile) and Mallard Slough Trail (3.3 mile loop) begin at the Environmental Education Center. The marquee Alviso Loop Trail begins at Alviso Marina County Park, which offers a boat launch, two piers and boardwalks with great views of the mountains bordering the bay.

DIRECTIONS: From I-880 in San Jose, exit CA-237 toward Mountain View and drive west 2.4 miles. Exit on North First Street (which becomes North Taylor) and drive into Alviso. Turn right on Gold Street, left on Elizabeth Street and right on Hope Street to Alviso Marina County Park and a large parking lot.

THE HIKE: Walk northeast along the paved path that soon bends left and continues as a dirt road. Pass a viewing platform and follow Alviso Slough Trail north into the SFBNWR. Travel a levee dividing the salt ponds. (You'll know it when a train barrels down the tracks through the refuge!)

Chose one of two left turns; both equidistant (1.3 miles) trails merge eventually. Alviso Slough Trail bends south, then east between the edge of the bay on the right and the edge of the salt ponds on the left and returns to the marina.

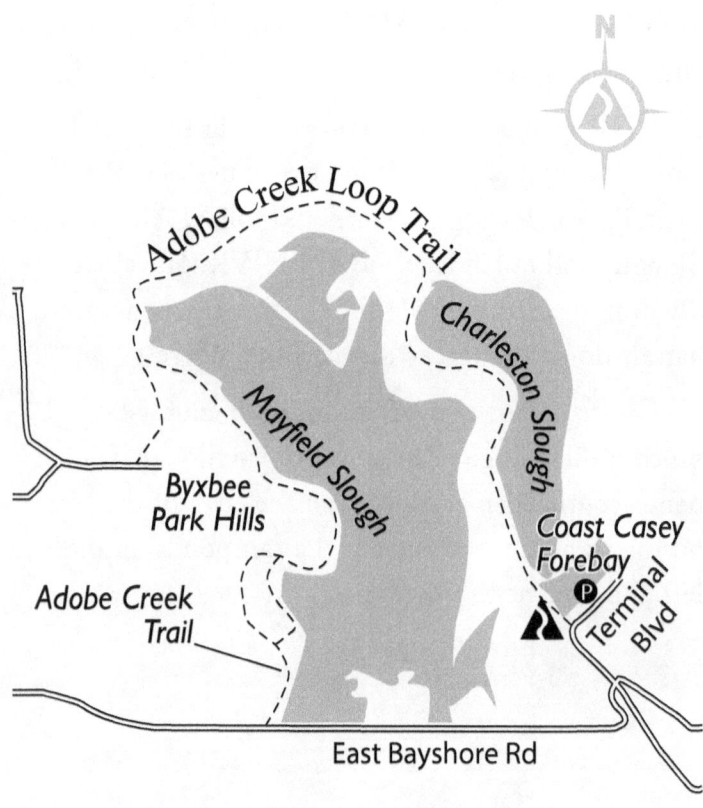

BAYLANDS PRESERVE
ADOBE CREEK LOOP TRAIL

5.6 miles round trip

Bird-watching is terrific at the Baylands, one of the West Coast's top birding areas. Millions of migratory birds arrive here as a destination or stopover as they travel the Pacific Flyway during spring and fall.

Spreading across nearly 2,000 acres, Palo Alto's Baylands Nature Preserve is one of the largest relatively natural salt marshes remaining on San Francisco Bay. The marsh was once even more extensive before being drained and divided repeatedly during the 19th and 20th centuries.

Squeezed between East Palo Alto and Mountain View, and bordered by an airport and wastewater treatment plant, the Baylands is a refuge in every sense of the word—for a multitude of birds, and for the many humans who come here to escape the stresses of modern life.

Preservation and restoration efforts have succeeded in making The Baylands a top quality preserve. Gone are the garbage trucks that for decades rumbled to the edge of the marsh. The city closed the Palo Alto Landfill and converted it into "Byxbee Park Hills," complete with re-vegetated slopes, benches, and trails.

The Baylands is a favorite exercise spot for locals for walks and runs along 15 miles of multi-use trail. Some describe the experience of traveling over the flat pathways across the marshland as "meditative" or "zen-like."

Choose from a variety of trails. San Francisquito Creek Trail (3.2 miles) is an out-and-back that begins in the shadow of Highway 101 and leads to the recently renovated Lucy Evans Baylands Nature Interpretive Center, built on pilings at the edge of the salt marsh. A plank boardwalk extends 0.25 mile across the marsh and serves up a grand view of San Francisco Bay.

Marsh Front Trail (1 mile) is a nature trail with numerous interpretive panels that highlight the unique habitat of the Baylands. Duck Pond Loop Trail (0.7 mile) is a favorite of children. In the 1930s the city of Palo Alto built a saltwater swimming pool (now the Duck Pond).

Hilltop Trails (3.5 miles or more) lead up and down hills created from the former landfill.

Adobe Creek Loop Trail (a segment of San Francisco Bay Trail) offers outstanding bird-watching opportunities and a fine tour of the Baylands.

DIRECTIONS: Join the loop from Terminal Boulevard by Mountain View's Shoreline Park or off Embarcadero in the Byxbee Park Hills section of the Baylands. Both trailheads offer free parking and restrooms. Another access is from the 3500 block of East Bayshore Road.

THE HIKE: From the Terminal Boulevard trailhead, the path leads north along the levee between Charleston Slough and Adobe Creek. The wide trail curves around San Francisco Bay, bends west, and crosses the tidal gate of Mayfield Slough at about the 2-mile mark. Look to the opposite shore and spot the Sailing Station dock. Wildlife-viewing stations line Mayfield Slough.

The trail turns southwest and with Byxbee Park Hills on the right and Matadero Creek on the left, travels to East Bay Shore Road. Walk east on a 0.75-mile length of paved trail (noisy and unpleasantly close to Highway 101) parallel to the road then another 0.4 mile of paved trail along Adobe Creek back to the trailhead.

Favorite exercise spot for zen-like walks, runs and hikes.

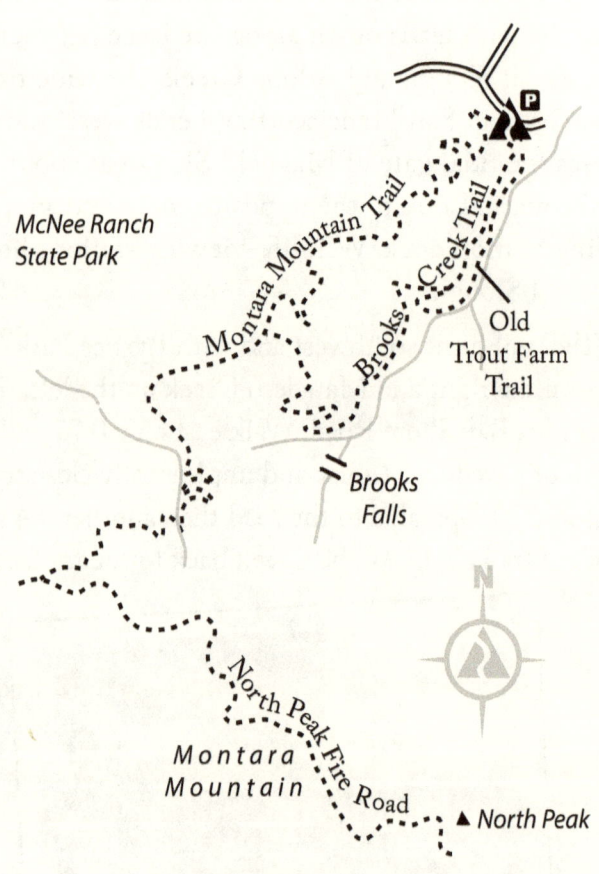

Montara Mountain

Montara Mountain, North Peak, Brooks Creek Trail

From San Pedro Valley County Park to Montara Mountain is 7 miles round trip with 1,200-foot elevation gain

Montara Mountain, perched above the San Mateo Coast just 10 miles south of San Francisco, offers grand views and wide open spaces. And oh, what a view! The coastline from Half Moon Bay to the Golden Gate National Recreation Area is at your feet.

The panoramic view is a hiker's reward for the rigorous ascent of Montara Mountain, whose slopes form the bulk of the McNee Ranch State Park. Montara Mountain, geologists say, is a 90-million-year-old chunk of granite (largely quartz diorite) that forms the northernmost extension of the Santa Cruz Mountains.

The coastal scrub community— ceanothus, sage and monkeyflower—predominates on the mountain.

One way up Montara Mountain is through McNee Ranch State Park from the coast, from McNee's sister state park, Montara State Beach, a half-mile long sand strand that's a popular surfing, fishing and picnicking spot. The park boasts several flower-strewn grasslands, and offers some great views, but it's quite a trek.

(BTW, what is a beautiful park to hikers and mountain bikers has long been considered an ideal location for a multi-lane highway by the California Department of Transportation. Caltrans has suggested building a Highway 1 bypass through the park to replace the existing landslide-prone stretch of highway known as the Devil's Slide that begins about two miles south of Pacifica. Of course, Caltrans—and its building plans—has been fiercely contested by environmentalists!)

A better and more scenic way to hike up Montara Mountain is to start from adjacent San Pedro Valley County Park, which offers water, restrooms, and a picnic area. Exhibits at the park visitor center highlight the mountain's flora and wildlife (lots of bobcats around here!), and there's even a little gift/bookstore.

DIRECTIONS: From Highway 1 in Pacifica, some 9 miles south of San Francisco (the junction of I-280 and 19th Ave), turn inland on Linda Mar Boulevard and head east 2 miles to Oddstad Boulevard. Turn right and there's the entry to San Pedro Valley County Park (fee) on your left.

THE HIKE: Ascend Montara Mountain Trail through a eucalyptus woodland sprinkled with such natives as ceanothus, coffeeberry and monkeyflower. Enjoy ocean vistas, including the Golden Gate Bridge and Mt. Tam near the 1.2-mile mark and the junction with Brooks Creek Trail (your return route.)

Continue the climb on switchbacks and nearly two miles along, enter the state park. After another 0.4 mile, turn left on wide North Peak Fire Road, which climbs moderately then more steeply. The fire road flattens out near the summit, topped with radio towers. Vistas from the slopes and fire road include the wide Pacific to the west and Mt. Diablo to the east.

Retrace your steps to Brooks Creek Trail (5.8 miles along) and bear right, descending into a lushly vegetated canyon. A trailside bench offers a view of Brook Creek Falls, a pretty little three-tiered falls that's usually more a trickle than a cascade. Continue the descent amidst a mixture of oak, pine, and redwood to the picnic area and trailhead.

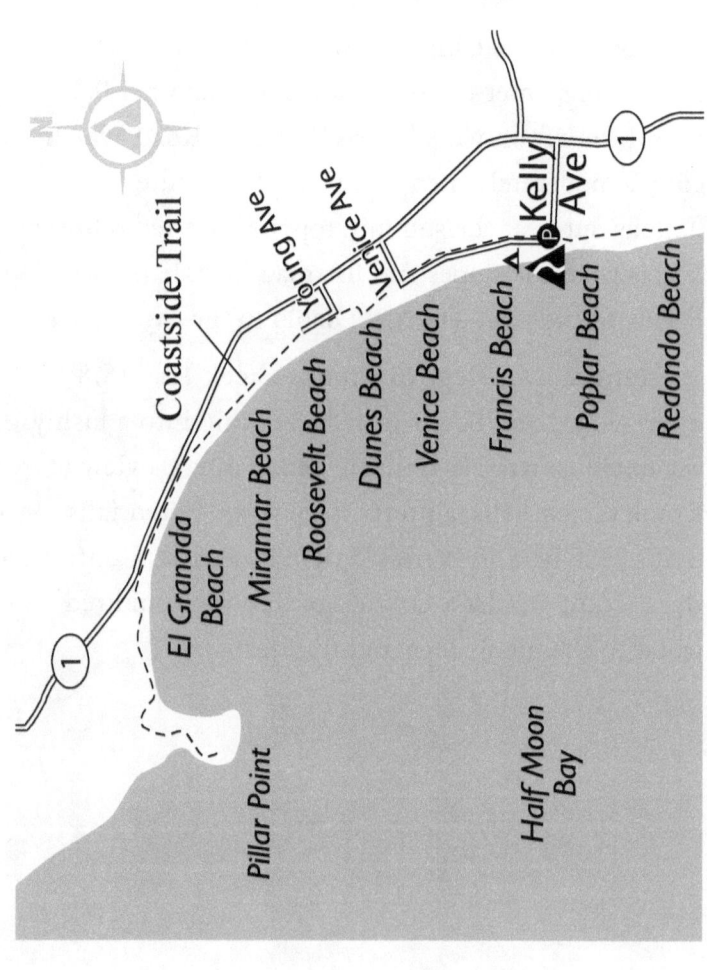

Half Moon Bay State Park
Coastside Trail

From Francis Beach to Roosevelt Beach is 6 miles round trip

Located only a half hour away from the San Mateo Bridge, Half Moon Bay is a distinct contrast to suburbia: pumpkin patches color the fields just out of town orange in autumn; the town with its unusual crafts shops and seafood cafés; and especially the beach.

From East Breakwater, Half Moon Bay arcs southward, backed by a long sandy beach. Forming a backdrop to the beach are eroded cliffs and low dunes.

Coastside Trail, part of the California Coastal Trail, extends 9 miles along Half Moon Bay from Purisima Creek south of the Ritz-Carlton Hotel all the way to Pillar Point Harbor. The trail is used by hikers and bicyclists (some portions are paved and wheelchair accessible).

The middle third of the trail crosses the three miles of shoreline and four beaches—Roosevelt, Dunes, Venice and Francis—that comprise Half

Moon Bay State Park. Coastside Trail puts these marvelous beaches within reach.

Want more? From the north end of the park continue your walk by beachcombing northward toward Pillar Harbor by way of Miramar Beach and El Granada Beach.

Extending south of the state park is more accessible—and walkable—shoreline.

Whether you're looking for a family day at the beach or a more romantic visit timed for one of the fabulous Half Moon Bay sunsets, the state park is a great place to go.

And hike. The trail winds past low sandy hills, dotted by clumps of cord-grass.

Watch for whales, in fact pods of whales, swimming by.

DIRECTIONS: From Highway 1 in the town of Half Moon Bay (0.25 mile north of the intersection with Highway 92) turn west on Kelly Avenue and drive to Francis Beach. There is a state park day use fee.

THE HIKE: Begin at Francis Beach, the most popular spot for a day at the beach with large parking lots (that fill up quickly on sunny weekends and holidays), plenty of barbecue grills and picnic tables. The park's southernmost beach is a classic: wide and sandy, with a grassy picnic area that borders the park's popular campground.

From Francis Beach, hike north to rather secluded Elmar Beach, where Pilarcitos Creek empties into the ocean. When the creek pools up behind the sands, it forms a wetlands that's great habitat for the birds but can make it a challenge to access this beach—best done by way of a long footbridge.

Hike on to sandy Venice Beach, which lies between Pilarcitos Creek on south and Frenchman's Creek in the north. From atop sandstone bluffs, descend short, steep, sandy trails to Dunes Beach.

Turnaround point for this hike is Roosevelt (aka Naples) Beach in the northwest part of the park, north of "downtown" and adjacent to the Miramar neighborhood.

Hike Coastside Trail to the lovely beaches along Half Moon Bay.

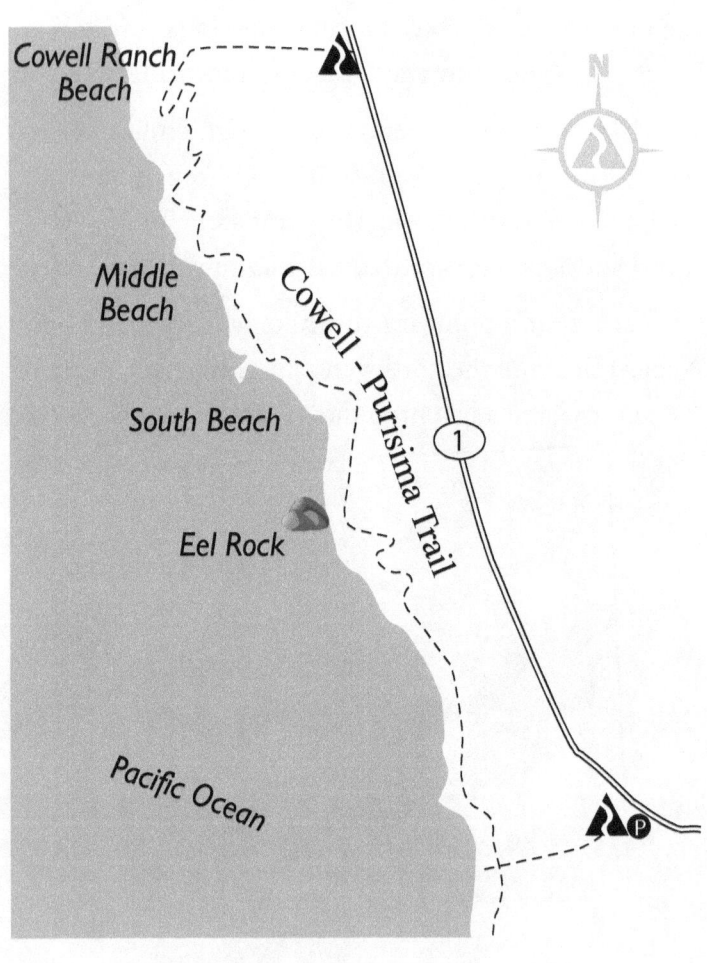

Cowell Ranch Beach
Cowell-Purisima Trail

From North Trailhead to Overlook is 1 mile round trip; to South Overlook is 6.6 miles round trip

Enjoy spectacular San Mateo Coast panoramas from cliff-top promontories along Cowell-Purisima Trail. The trail leads along the edge of tall bluffs south of Half Moon Bay, and delivering views of harbor seals on the beach and in the waters below.

A portion of the California Coastal Trail, Cowell-Purisima Trail is an example of government and private landholders working together to secure easements across farmland and create a length of coastal trail. The California Coastal Conservancy and Peninsula Open Space Trust spearheaded the project and it wasn't easy: the trail, which opened in 2011, took 25 years of work and a million dollars a mile to build!

Cowell-Purisima Trail is open to both hikers and bicyclists and is open only on weekends and federal holidays. North and south trailheads offer parking, restrooms and interpretive displays that highlight the coastal environment and local farming.

Join the trail by first hiking to a bluff-top overlook above two beaches. Seal Beach, south of the overlook, is a preserve for harbor seals and closed to public access. A 0.25-mile long sandy beach lies north of the overlook and is accessible via a steep staircase.

DIRECTIONS: From its junction with Route 92 in Half Moon Bay, follow Highway 1 south 3 miles to a parking lot on the (right) ocean side of Highway 1. To reach the southern trailhead for Cowell Purisima Trail, continue 2 more miles to a parking area on the right.

THE HIKE: Walk west on the wide dirt road. Interpretive displays on this length of trail identify the local plants and wildlife and provide local history lessons.

The trail crosses the onetime route of Ocean Shores Railroad, which ran between the hamlet of Tunitas Glen 8 miles south of Half Moon Bay to San Francisco. The railroad operated from 1908 until 1920; it was forced to close when Highway 1 was completed and travelers opted for cars.

At 0.3 mile, past a left fork with Cowell-Purisima Trail, and at 0.4 mile a right fork with a stairway to Cowell Ranch Beach. After 0.5 mile, the trail ends at a fenced overlook. The harbor seals are most visible from February to May, and particularly fascinating during March and April, when pups are born.

Retrace your steps to Cowell-Purisima Trail and hike north on the wide path across fields that have been farmed more than a century. Get great photo ops of the pocket beaches and seals below, and inland across the fields to the foothills of the Santa Cruz Mountains.

Three well constructed bridges en route help make the going even easier. About the only elevation change occurs halfway into the hike, when the trail switchbacks down into a ravine and crosses a bridge over Purisima Creek.

Reach an overlook at the south end of the trail and enjoy inspiring vistas of Half Moon Bay and beyond. (The trail swings inland and leads to a parking lot on Highway 1.)

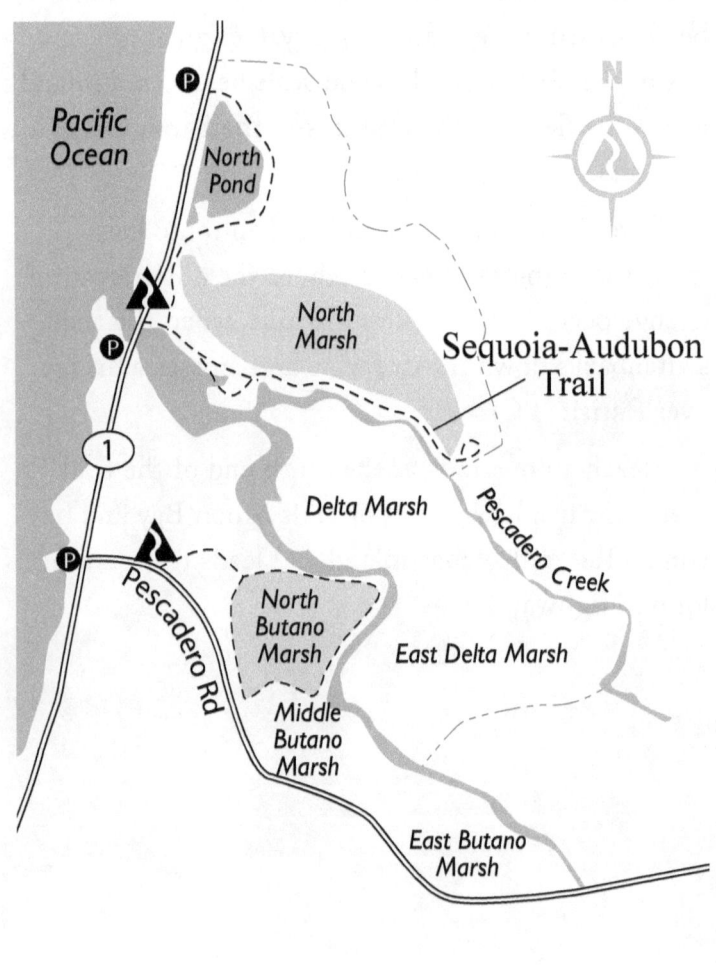

Pescadero Marsh

Sequoia Audubon Trail

From Pescadero State Beach to North Marsh is 2.5 miles round trip; to North Pond is 2.5 miles round trip

Bring a pair of field glasses to Pescadero Marsh Natural Preserve, the largest marsh between Monterey Bay and San Francisco. Pescadero Creek and Butano Creek pool resources to form a lagoon and estuary that is a haven for birds, and a heaven for birdwatchers.

Peer through willows, tules and cattails, and you might spot diving ducks, great egrets, or yellow-throated warblers. More than 180 species of birds have been sighted in the preserve.

Best birding is in late fall and early spring. To protect the birds during breeding season, the northernmost preserve trail is closed. You may take one of the walks described below, or simply wander the perimeter of the marsh to one of the wooden observation decks, and begin your bird-watching.

DIRECTIONS: Pescadero State Beach and Pescadero Marsh Natural Preserve are located off Highway 1, some 15 miles south of Half Moon Bay. The state beach has three parking areas. The central parking lot is the trailhead for Sequoia Audubon Trail. (The largest parking area is at the south end of the beach, where Pescadero Road junctions Highway 1.)

THE HIKE: From the inland side of the parking lot, take a wooden staircase to a pedestrian walkway along the Highway 1 Bridge. Reach a staircase and descend to the beach. From the beach, walk under the bridge to reach the lagoon and Sequoia Audubon Trail.

The trail meanders between the south shore of North Marsh and the north bank of Butano Creek. Take the first fork to the left and loop toward North Marsh. A right turn, as you near the marsh, will allow you to loop back to the Sequoia Audubon Trail.

To North Pond: (North Pond Trail begins across the highway from the northern state beach parking lot or from Sequoia Audubon Trail.) Follow the 0.5 mile path as it loops around North Pond and check out the abundant birdlife that populates the surrounding thickets. The path climbs a small hill where a wooden observation deck affords a grand view of the large North Marsh.

You can return by taking the trail south and to the left. It leads to Sequoia Audubon Trail, which in turn takes you under the Butano Creek Bridge. You then follow the beach back to your starting point.

Butano Trail:(trailhead on Pescadero Road just off Highway 1) The trail leads north from the parking area, and winds through a wide, lush meadow. When you get to the creek, follow the trail east (right-ward).

As you follow Butano Creek, you'll be walking the tops of dikes that allow coastal farmers to use this rich bottomland for growing artichokes, Brussels sprouts, and beans. Watch for blue herons and snowy egrets. After following Butano Creek through the marsh, you'll join the trail to the right to return to the starting point.

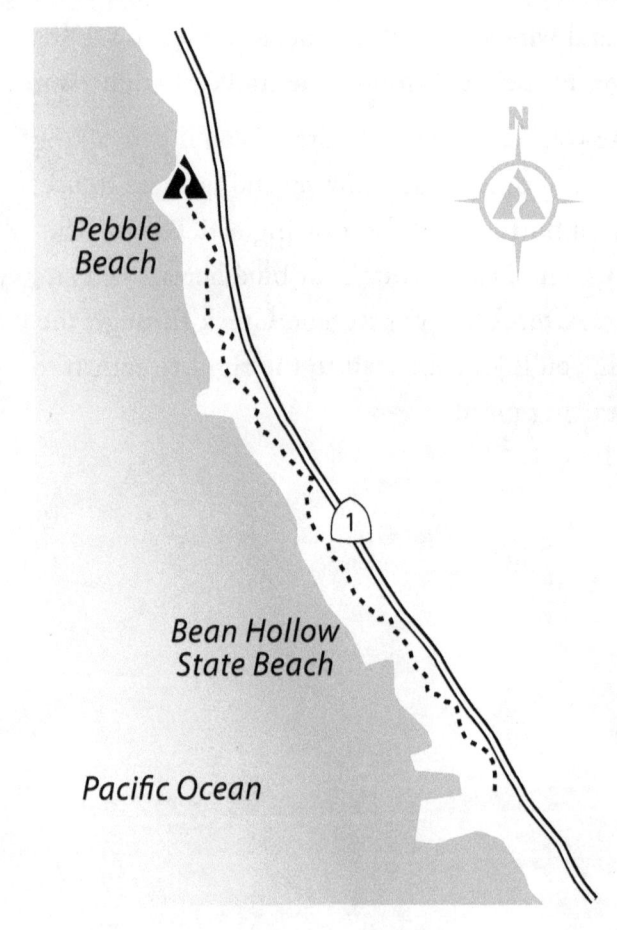

BEAN HOLLOW STATE BEACH
Arroyo de los Frijoles Trail

From Pebble Beach to Bean Hollow Beach is 2 miles round trip

If you're driving 55 mph or so along Highway 1 and look out at Bean Hollow Beach, you might not notice anything that distinguishes it from other beaches. Stop. Take a second look. Take a hike.

Bean Hollow State Beach is one of the more intriguing San Mateo County beaches that extend from Ano Nuevo State Park to Thornton State Beach, a bit south of San Francisco. Some travelers say that the San Mateo County beaches and bluffs remind them of the British coast near Cornwall.

Arroyo de los Frijoles, "Creek of the Beans," empties into Lake Lucerne, just east of Pacific Coast Highway. The state beach originally had the Spanish name before being Americanized to Bean Hollow. Picnic tables at the beach suggest a lunch or rest stop.

This exploration begins at Bean Hollow Beach's northern end, at Pebble Beach—not to be confused with the Pebble Beach of 18-hole renown near Carmel, the Pebble Beach in Tomales Bay State Park, or the Pebble Beach near Crescent City…no kidding it's a common name! Anyway, the pebbles on this Pebble Beach are quartz chipped from an offshore reef, tumbled ashore, then wave-polished and rounded into beautifully hued "beans:" agate, moonstone, chert, jasper and jade.

The one-mile walk between Bean Hollow State Beach and Pebble Beach offers a close-up look at tidepools, wildflowers (in season), and colonies of harbor seals and shorebirds. The rocky intertidal area is habitat for sea slugs, snails, crabs, anemones and sea urchins..

Bird-watchers will sight cormorants, pelicans and red-billed oystercatchers flying over the water. The sandy beach is patrolled by gulls, sandpipers and sanderlings.

DIRECTIONS: Bean Hollow State Beach is located some 40 miles south of San Francisco. The beach is off Highway 1, about 3.5 miles south of Pescadero. The trail begins at the south end of the parking lot (fee). There is free parking along Highway 1.

THE HIKE: The first part of the walk is along a nature trail. Waves crashing over the offshore reef are a dramatic sight. Keep an eye out for harbor seals swimming just offshore. This north end of the beach displays the unusual "beans," gem-like rocks that are a wonder to behold. You just can't help scooping them up into your hands. (Touch them all you want, but don't keep them; collecting the stone is strictly forbidden.).

A couple of small footbridges aid your crossing of rivulets that carve the coastal bluffs. To the south, you'll get a glimpse of Pigeon Point Lighthouse, now part of a hostel. If the tide is low when you approach Bean Hollow State Beach, head down to the sand.

Arroyo de los Frijoles, "Creek of the Beans," empties into Lake Lucerne, just east of Pacific Coast Highway. The state beach originally had the Spanish name before being Americanized to Bean Hollow. Picnic tables at the beach suggest a lunch or rest stop, and good place to pause for a moment to give thanks for the foresight of those who preserved Bean Hollow as a California State Park back in 1958.

How Bean Hollow Beach got its name: From the "beans," wave-polished stones that wash ashore.

Discover More Day Hikes and Bay Hikes!

HIKE THE EAST BAY
Best Day Hikes in the East Bay's Parks,
Preserves and Special Places

HIKE SAN FRANCISCO
Best Day Hikes in the Golden Gate
National Parklands and Around the City

HIKE POINT REYES
Best Day Hikes in
Point Reyes National Seashore

THETRAILMASTER.COM

- Tips
- Tours
- Trails
- Tales

JOHN MCKINNEY

John McKinney is an award-winning writer, public speaker, and author of 30 hiking-themed books: inspiring narratives, top-selling guides, books for children.

John is particularly passionate about sharing the stories of California trails. He is the only one to have visited—and written about—all 280 California State Parks. John tells the story of his epic hike along the entire California coast in the critically acclaimed *Hiking on the Edge: Dreams, Schemes, and 1600 Miles on the California Coastal Trail.*

For 18 years John, aka The Trailmaster, wrote a weekly hiking column for the Los Angeles Times, and has hiked and enthusiastically told the story of more than 10 thousand miles of trail across California and around the world. His "Every Trail Tells a Story" series of guides highlight the very best hikes in California.

The intrepid Eagle Scout has written more than a thousand stories and opinion pieces about hiking, parklands, and our relationship with nature.

A passionate advocate for hiking and our need to reconnect with nature, John is a frequent public speaker, and shares his tales on radio, on video, and online.

JOHN MCKINNEY:
"EVERY TRAIL TELLS A STORY."

HIKE ON.

TheTrailmaster.com

www.ingramcontent.com/pod-product-compliance
Lightning Source LLC
Chambersburg PA
CBHW030445300426
44112CB00009B/1165